I Remember...When God Showed Up

A Journey of Faith

Denise E. King

WESTBOW
P R E S S®
A DIVISION OF THOMAS NELSON
& ZONDERVAN

THE HOLY BIBLE, NEW INTERNATIONAL VERSION®, NIV® Copyright © 1973, 1978, 1984, 2011 by Biblica, Inc.® Used by permission. All rights reserved worldwide. Scripture taken from the King James Version of the Bible.

Song lyrics, "I'll Make the Darkness Light," Charles P. Jones, 1916

This book is a work of non-fiction. Unless otherwise noted, the author and the publisher make no explicit guarantees as to the accuracy of the information contained in this book and in some cases, names of people and places have been altered to protect their privacy.

WestBow Press books may be ordered through booksellers or by contacting:

WestBow Press
A Division of Thomas Nelson & Zondervan
1663 Liberty Drive
Bloomington, IN 47403
www.westbowpress.com
1 (866) 928-1240

Because of the dynamic nature of the Internet, any web addresses or links contained in this book may have changed since publication and may no longer be valid. The views expressed in this work are solely those of the author and do not necessarily reflect the views of the publisher, and the publisher hereby disclaims any responsibility for them.

Any people depicted in stock imagery provided by Thinkstock are models, and such images are being used for illustrative purposes only. Certain stock imagery © Thinkstock.

ISBN: 978-1-9736-0717-5 (sc)
ISBN: 978-1-9736-0716-8 (hc)
ISBN: 978-1-9736-0718-2 (e)

Library of Congress Control Number: 2017917307

Print information available on the last page.

WestBow Press rev. date: 11/9/2017

Dedication

When I remember the countless, complicated, and consuming events of my life for which *God showed up* for me, I am in complete awe. I give God all the glory, honor, and the praise. Therefore, I dedicate this book to my Lord and Savior, Jesus Christ.

> Remember the former things of old: for I am God, and there is none else; I am God, and there is none like me, Declaring the end from the beginning, and from ancient times the things that are not yet done, saying, My counsel shall stand, and I will do all my pleasure. (Isaiah 46:9–10)

Acknowledgments

I want to acknowledge my family for their unending love and support during my entire life—my mom, Veola, and my sisters and brothers, Janice, Cecil Jr., Rickey (deceased), Vernita, Jerry, and Darren. You all are my rock. My love for you is immeasurable.

My mother taught me to strive for excellence, to have a voice, and not to settle for less. She has been my go-to, the one I lean on during my faith journey. God gave me the best in you to bring out the best in me. I thank God for you.

My big sister, Janice, is my best friend, with a heart that exceeds the heights of heaven. God used her to birth the title of this book during an early-morning conversation about God's amazing blessings in my life. Thank you for always listening and supporting my ideas, my hopes, and my dreams.

My big brother, Cecil Jr., has provided me support during some of the most difficult financial challenges in my life, and I thank God for him. He is extremely funny too. Many days I talked to him and laughed so hard that I forgot what was troubling me.

I honor the memory of my brother Rickey. On the day my brother was killed, he spoke a word to me that changed my life forever.

This book has been in the making for years because of my brother Jerry, who always encouraged me to "write the book." Well, I finally did it. Thank you for always encouraging me through the worst of days and the best of days. Your sacrifice and support are written in heaven.

My brother Darren has always supported my dreams and encouraged me to do what it takes. When I am weary and worn from the daily press, he pumps me up and sends me back into the game. I can stand strong in the face of adversity because of his strength.

Last, a special thank you to my sister, best friend, prayer partner, and prayer warrior, Vernita, who prayed me through during many of the times when God showed up. She speaks the word of God with power and an anointing that causes things to change. Thank you, my sister, for being true to your call and your faith.

I love you all and thank God for birthing me into this family. I remember when God showed up for me through all of you.

Contents

Introduction

I Remember...When God Showed Up: A Journey of Faith is written with you in mind. It is an effort to get more people to purposely remember God in everything, for everything, and in every way—to remember *who* God is, *what* God has already done, and *what* God is well able to do. As a result of remembering God, I hope that you will begin to give him praise, to let him know how much you appreciate him and how much you love him. In the end, I hope that your faith is increased and you can rely totally on God to handle the present challenges and situations in your life.

I also wrote this book because I needed to remind myself of what God has done in my life. I needed to remember my journey of faith, to encourage myself at this very present moment of my life. I needed to chronicle as much as I could recall because I often forget more than I remember. I forget the details of the things I encountered along this journey of life. I sometimes forget that the same God who brought me through *that* (that thing in the past) is the same God who can bring me through *this* (the challenge or issue I am dealing with right now).

What I found was that the more I remember about what God has already done, the more I am encouraged in my faith and trust in God to bring me through this present difficulty. I find peace, hope, joy, and strength to not just make it through but to conquer!

Now, let me add some clarity about the phrase *when God showed up*. God is omnipresent. He is everywhere, and there is no place that he is not. God is omnipotent. He is able to do anything, and he cannot fail. God is omniscient. He is all-knowing. There is nothing known that God does not know. Therefore, God knows exactly what we are going through. God knows the answer or solution to every challenge we face. God is able to bring us through every crisis, every challenge, and every struggle. Nothing, absolutely nothing, is too hard for God. So I do not want anyone confused about the phrase *when God showed up*. He is there at all times. This phrase was simply meant to show the magnificent ways in which God answers our prayers or brings us through situations and circumstances that we face on a daily basis.

I know what God has done in my life but always thought it did not warrant me writing about it. I wrote this book in obedience to God and through the encouragement of my brother and sister. My obedience did not come right away or overnight but was years in the making. Many times I sat down to write and immediately got distracted by the smallest things.

I laugh about it now because I understand that anything that brings God glory is often met with challenges—great and small. You were made to bring God glory. Therefore, your life may be challenged right now, while you're reading this book. Nonetheless, I encourage you to remember what God has already done in your life. Remember the times when God brought you through a situation that seemed impossible. Remember when God did something that no man could have ever done or when God used someone to do what no one else was able or willing to do for you. Remember God. Remember that he is the almighty God, the great I Am, the faithful God. Put it in perspective. Make it personal. Don't try to remember what God did for someone else, but rather remember what God did for *you*.

I guarantee you there is a long list of things you can recall. In case you are having a hard time remembering, here is a short list of what God has done—today.

You woke up this morning. Who woke you up? Nope, it was not your spouse, child, pet, or the alarm clock. God allowed you to see another day, a new day, a day you have never seen before and shall never see again.

You have the ability to see, hear, speak, walk, dress yourself, or feed yourself. Who made it possible? God did it. It does not matter if you use assistance in doing any of these things. What is important is that you're still able to do them.

You have a job or source of income. Who provided the resources? Yes, it was God.

You have shelter, a roof over your head. Who provided for you? Again I say it was God. I think you get it now.

This may be news to some of you, but the power of your own hand did not bring these blessings to you. Your job did not bring these blessings to you, *and* it is not because you are so smart, talented, pretty, handsome, or rich either.

I think that if we begin to read and apply God's word to our situations, we will begin to see the power of God's word in a new way, a way that transforms our thinking and therefore transforms us from worry, doubt, and fear to faith, hope, and power.

God is in your situation. He is there, waiting for you, for me, for us to seek him for help, to trust him for help, and to obey his direction. It is not so much that God shows up. Remember, he is always there. It is actually that we begin to *see* him when we begin to trust him and have faith in him to handle whatever we are facing. When we remember God, we see that God is bigger than our situations. We see that God is faithful to honor his word. He promised never to leave us without help or hope and to never forsake us.

It is my prayer that you will begin and continue to remember God—who he is and what he has done in your life—as you read the testimonies of my life. Perhaps you have similar testimonies and will therefore find yourself on the same path at times. Whatever your experience in reading these pages, it is my sincere belief that you too will begin to see how God was there all along and how he showed up for you time and time again. I pray that this journey of faith stirs your memory until praise bursts forth from your belly through your lips and God is glorified.

Remember to share your testimonies with others. You may never know how your experience may be the very instrument

God uses to bring someone through a difficult situation. Be blessed, and remember when God showed up for you!

And they overcame him by the blood of the Lamb, and by the word of their testimony. (Revelation 12:11a KJV)

Chapter 1

HE KNEW ME BEFORE

Before I formed thee in the belly I knew thee;
and before thou camest forth out of the womb
I sanctified thee, and I ordained thee a prophet
unto the nations.

—Jeremiah 1:5

God knew you before you were formed in your mother's womb.
He knows the plans that he has for you, and he wants you to trust
him. He is a patient God who longs for a relationship with you.

It amazes me when I remember my life before Christ and see
how God was yet blessing and providing for me. Whenever I talk
or think about my childhood, it is always with fond recall. My
brothers and I can talk for hours on end about our upbringing

and how it shaped us as adults. Most times we laugh so hard and long about some of the stuff we used to do and how much fun we had as kids. It is not unusual for us to reenact the stories of our childhood during family gatherings, which makes us and others laugh so hard that we cannot speak or are literally on the floor with uncontrollable outbursts of thunderous laughter and tears streaming down our faces. (I'm laughing right now at the thought of it.)

My mother raised seven children, and I am the sixth child, the youngest girl. My older siblings looked out for me since I was a young girl growing up in our low-income housing community (often referred to as the projects). I was five years old when we moved in. They were still building some of the apartment units at the time. Over time, the community changed and became known as a very rough neighborhood—one of the toughest areas in the city. Drugs, crime, and many other dangerous activities ran rampant in the neighborhood. However, many of the families there formed a close-knit community that looked out for each other and made sure the children were protected.

My brothers were my protectors and made sure the boys in the neighborhood didn't get "out of line" with me. My sisters made sure we kept the house clean and that I had the necessities a growing girl needed. Along with our neighbors, we took pride in keeping the grassy areas and sidewalks leading to our apartments clean and clutter free. My mother kept us all in line—even the neighborhood kids. She didn't "play" and didn't allow the "anything goes" mind-set in her house. She demanded respect and gave us respect as well. We have many stories about when one of us crossed the line with her and how she quickly straightened us out. Oh, the stories!

I refer to my mother as the matriarch of the family. My mother always believed in and supported her family. At almost eighty years old, she still remembers everybody's birthday, sends a daily text message of a scripture or a word of encouragement, makes daily calls to so many people to encourage them in their faith, and tends to the sick to make sure they receive adequate medical care and knowledge to address their issues. She can sing with such skill that it causes your cares to subside and your heart to be lifted up. She has a laugh that is contagious and that will make you stop and laugh, even if you are not in the same room or in the same conversation. She is a fierce businesswoman and a no-nonsense kind of person. She is my mother and a mother to many whom she did not birth. God chose her to bring me into this world, and for that I am eternally grateful. I have learned so much from my mother that this book could never contain.

God had his hand on my mother and gave her the strength and desire to take care of her children in a way that has been the catalyst for who I have become as a young lady, as a woman of God, and as a businesswoman.

My mother worked hard to provide for her children. I remember how often she worked double shifts at the hospital (11:00 p.m. to 7:00 a.m., and then 7:00 a.m. to 3:00 p.m. or vice versa). She was always meticulously dressed in her white uniform and taught us the importance of presenting your best self on the job. Even as a kid, I was always amazed at how my mother managed to work sixteen-hour shifts. I would later come to realize that I inherited that hardworking, do-what-it-takes approach from my mother when my career demanded the same.

I remember my mother working those long shifts and yet coming home to cook for her kids. I remember the days of plenty, yet I remember the days of rumbling through the cabinets and refrigerator over and over again, wondering, hoping, but then being creative with a mix of this and a mix of that—anything to settle the hunger. I can now say that I am grateful for the days of scarcity because they taught me how to trust God for greater, for better, and for more.

When I was in the third grade, I wanted to take piano lessons after school. My brother and I stayed for the first class. I was bubbling with excitement because I wanted to learn how to play the piano, and it seemed that I would do just that. However, the teacher started asking each child for their twenty-dollar fee for the six-week course. We did not have the money. The teacher told us that we could not stay because our parents could not afford to pay. We were asked to leave the class before she could begin, and she waited and watched us leave. I didn't want to leave. I wanted to stay. I wanted to learn to play the piano—that was all!

Children don't handle disappointment well at all, and neither did I. As we gathered our things, I remember trying to hold back my tears so the other kids would not see me cry. I made it to the door and suddenly the floodgates opened. I cried the entire walk home. My brother tried to console me, but it was to no avail. He kept saying that it was all right and not to cry. The more I thought about it, the more I cried. All I could say was, "Why couldn't we stay? She could have allowed us to stay the first day and then tell us after class, away from the other kids." I certainly didn't expect to be put out of the class and sent home in tears. How did she know what my parents could afford? I was embarrassed and disappointed. It took me days to get over it.

As a little eight-year-old girl, humiliation and shame were new to me, especially when incited by an adult. However, these feelings did not linger long, because another emotion—anger—showed up shortly thereafter. When I went back to school, I remember thinking the teacher didn't want me in her class and that's why we were asked to leave. It made me mad.

I think the anger was good for me because it pushed me beyond the shame and into a place within myself that said, *I can do anything I put my mind to, and nothing will stop me.* As a kid, this is a really powerful position because there are no fears or other showstoppers that prevent us from achieving our dreams. At that moment, I decided that I would excel in anything that I set out to do! As a third grader, my goal was to make straight As on my report card. That's funny to me now, because that was the extent of my anger or the "I'll show that teacher" attitude. Well, that mind-set would catapult me to higher academic levels my entire time through grammar, high school, college, and even graduate school. It was a mind-set! God knew what it would take to push me to levels that I perhaps would not have ever reached or even cared to reach.

That third-grade experience stayed with me and also made me more sensitive to the needs of disadvantaged youths. It made me keenly aware of how important it is to encourage young people, especially disadvantaged youths, to pursue their dreams. I became more determined in my quest to achieve and help others experience things they never thought they could do—or have, for that matter. It also taught me to never allow money or the lack thereof to hinder me from pursuing my dreams and desires.

Perhaps that teacher didn't mean any harm that day—at least I would like to think so. Nonetheless, it made me more consciously aware of what I say to young people about their hopes and dreams and how I say it. I try to look for ways to encourage and support the ideas they share.

By the way, I never developed a musical skill. I am not musically inclined to this day. I cannot play an instrument or even sing (well, I think my voice is quite melodious, especially when I'm in the shower!). I love listening to music, but that is as far as it goes. Maybe that was God's way of saying he was saving me for something else—and it was not playing the piano.

The feelings of disappointment, humiliation, and shame are real and can be lasting for adults and especially for young children. We remember and hold on to these feelings without realizing the negative effect and toll they take on us—on our future, our success, and our happiness. Through God's help, we can move past these feelings and receive what God has for us, which is better than anything we can ever imagine. Remember— before we were formed, God knew us and the plans he has for us. The thing we desire a great deal may not be the thing that God has in his plans for us. God has something better and more fitting that positions us to become who he intended from the beginning.

I am so glad that even before I knew or acknowledged God's sovereign power in my life, he was still shielding and protecting me and my future. I know personally that words have power— even negative words. Now is the time to start speaking what God says about you. Leave the past in the past, and begin dealing with your present so you can positively impact your future.

If you are experiencing difficulty in getting beyond past disappointments or shame, begin to seek God for deliverance so you can be healed and released from it. He stands ready to move you from that place and into a place of freedom and peace. It is not a hard thing for God to help you through whatever it is, no matter how long ago it happened.

We often think that our situations are different from everyone else's and that nobody has ever dealt with the same. The enemy wants us to think that our situations are beyond help. That is far from the truth. Just know that God can and will strengthen you to rise above whatever has held you down, held you back, or caused you to stand still. You can move past this because God knew you before you were formed. He knows the plans he has for you. Don't let your past hold you back. Be released from it today.

Fear thou not, for I am with thee; be not dismayed, for I am thy God; I will strengthen thee, I will help thee, yea, I will uphold thee with the right hand of my righteousness. (Isaiah 41:10)

Chapter 2

I'M SAVED

But Jesus said, Suffer little children, and forbid
them not, to come unto me: for of such is the
kingdom of heaven.

—Matthew 19:14

I love to see children praising God—no inhibitions, no worries,
and no concern for who's watching. Parents, I encourage you to
set an atmosphere of praise and worship for your children from
the time they are born. It is one of the most positive and lasting
influences you can make.

For as long as I can remember, my mother was saved and had
a personal relationship with the Lord. Although she was not saved
her entire life, I can only remember her as a saved woman. Her

life in Christ set the foundation for me. I remember my mother talking about the Lord often. She prayed over our needs and often told us about the grace and mercy of God. I loved hearing her sing Christian songs. One of my favorite memories is playing outside, near the kitchen window, where I could hear her singing the songs that played on the radio. Sometimes I would just stand still to hear her sing—and of course smell the delicious food she was cooking. I love hearing her sing to this day. Her voice calms everything that concerns me.

While I was not saved growing up, I remember going to church with my mother. Just as some kids, I didn't want to go to church, especially a night service. I wanted to stay outside and play with the other children in the neighborhood. However, the more I went, the more I enjoyed going and the more I wanted to go.

When I was about twelve years old, I went to a summer tent revival with my mother. I remember it as a hot and muggy day, and all I thought about was being home playing outside with the other kids. However, my attention turned to what the preacher was saying. I don't remember all he preached about, but I do remember feeling like he was talking directly to me.

At the end of that service, I gave my life to Jesus and received him as my Lord and Savior. I didn't know how to feel. I just knew that the preacher was talking about me when he made the altar call. I remember feeling a bit awkward walking to the front of the church with all the adults who were going, some of them shouting and some crying too. I didn't understand it all, but I always remembered seeing people cry a lot when they walked to the front of the church. I felt good. I felt different but couldn't explain it. I didn't know what to expect. I just knew something was different about me.

When I got home, I was excited to tell the others that I was "saved." My excitement soon dissipated like a puff of smoke once the neighborhood kids started making fun of me. They called me all kinds of names. You may have heard a few of them—holy roller, sanctified, church girl, etc. They teased me unmercifully. I felt so embarrassed and ridiculed about being saved that I went behind one of the apartment buildings and literally started cursing, actually cussing out loud, although no one else was around. I didn't even know how to curse. I was making up words; none of it made any sense. I just thought that if I started using profanity, it would prove that I was not saved. I didn't understand that what other people thought really didn't matter. It was about me and Jesus, but I didn't know that I would be mocked for believing in Jesus or sharing my salvation with others. However, as a child, I couldn't bear the ongoing jokes from the neighborhood kids or others that I thought I would have to face.

Every day I started telling myself that I was not saved and how I did not want to be a "holy-roller." I thought that if I was saved as a child, I would not be able to have fun with the other kids or I would have to go to church every day.

I think about it now and honestly laugh at myself. How silly it all seems now. On the other hand, it makes me a bit sad because God was calling me and I answered briefly, but didn't come to him completely. I look back on that moment and now see the patience and mercy of God. I am not sure how different my life would be had I lived for Christ at an early age, but I can certainly say that once I gave my life to Christ, it was the best decision of my life! My only regret is that I didn't say yes to Christ sooner.

I am so glad God knew me better than I knew myself. God knew he would call me again and one day I would answer. I thank God for not giving up on me that day and many days, months, and years after that. Just the thought of God never giving up on me blesses my soul. God gave me another chance, another opportunity, and another open door to walk through to him. He did not abandon that little girl who abandoned him—cussing all the while behind that apartment building. Whew ... now that's good news!

Isn't it amazing how we can listen to the voice of others and not the voice of God? How quickly we believe what others say about us and not what God says about us. How do you dispel what others say about you? How do you know what to believe? The answer to these questions is simple, but not easy. It is knowing and trusting the word of God, reading and studying his word until we become what God says. That's simple, but it is not easy to stay before the Lord and to continue in his word because of the many distractions that try to (and often do) hinder our efforts. However, God desires to commune with us, to teach us what we need to know about him and about ourselves. To dispel untruths spoken by others, we must know the truth God has spoken.

Perhaps you said yes to God too but soon found yourself uncertain of your salvation due to the influence of others or for other reasons. God is yet waiting for you to completely surrender to him and be released from what others think.

For those who have hesitated to respond to the call of the Lord for some reason, I implore you to come to Christ Jesus. It will be the best decision of your life. Jesus will literally change your life. He will change your heart. I don't care how old you are or how long you have delayed in coming to Christ. God is waiting patiently for you, right now. He wants a relationship with you through his son, Jesus Christ. If you want to give your life to Christ, you can do so today, right now, right here. All you have to do is repeat the following prayer out loud and believe it in your heart:

Heavenly Father, I come to you in the name of your Son, Jesus Christ. You said in your word that whosoever shall call upon the name of the Lord shall be saved (Romans 10:13). Father, I am calling on Jesus right now. I believe that Jesus suffered and died on the cross for my sins. I believe Jesus was raised from the dead and he's alive right now. I believe Jesus hears me as I pray to him right now. Lord Jesus, I ask you now to come into my heart. Live your life in me and through me. I repent of my sins and surrender myself totally and completely to you. Heavenly Father, by faith, I now confess Jesus Christ as my Lord and Savior from this day forward. I dedicate my life to serving him.

Praise the Lord! Heaven is rejoicing! Once you have given your life to Christ, it is important that you find a church home where you can learn, fellowship, and grow in Christ. Ask the Lord to lead and guide you to where he wants you to attend church services. Get a good Bible, one that is easy for you to read and understand. Pray and ask God to give you understanding of his word and help you to apply his word to your everyday life. You will begin to see changes. Be patient with yourself and with others too. God is working things out for you.

I am so glad that you took this faith journey with me. I can only tell you that God is walking with you too. He knows what he has in store for you. You are his creation—a wonderful, marvelous creation.

I will praise thee; for I am fearfully and wonderfully made: marvellous are thy works; and that my soul knoweth right well. (Psalm 139:14)

Chapter 3

SUDDEN LOSS

Blessed are they that mourn: for they shall be comforted.

—Matthew 5:4

I believe everyone has felt some sense of loss about someone or something. It could be the death of a loved one, the breakup of a relationship, the loss of a job, or even the loss of something of value—a home, car, or pet. Anything we once loved and lost can bring a sense of grief and mourning that sometimes runs deeper than we could have ever imagined. The good news is that God is able to comfort all hurt and all sorrow.

It was a Sunday, May 17, four days before my seventeenth birthday. The night before was normal. I was babysitting my three young nieces, ages two, four, and six, for my sister and talking on the phone into the wee hours of the morning, until there was a knock on the door. It was not good news. As a matter of fact, it was terrible news. My brother Rickey had been shot, and things did not look good. It did not seem real at first. I was just with him. He had picked me up and taken me to my sister's house to babysit just hours before.

Was this really happening? What happened? This was my big brother, my protector, the one I came running home to one day when I was thirteen years old because some guy at the corner store had touched me inappropriately. This was the same brother who, when he heard it, jumped out of the shower, still soaking wet, put dry clothes on a wet body, and went to confront this guy. It was the same brother who told every single guy hanging out at the corner store to never look my way again and never think about putting their hands on me. (Well, he had some choice words while he was saying it.) It was the same brother who beat the guy up and honestly would have killed him had my younger brothers not intervened. After that, I never had any problems with any of the guys in the neighborhood; the word got out. It couldn't be my brother!

Just hours before the news, I was riding in the car with my brother. During the drive, our conversation was normal at first, and then his tone shifted. In the past, my brother always complained about how much it cost my mother to support my school activities—being a majorette, being in various clubs, travel costs, and school fees—that she could not afford. This time he did not fuss about it. He actually began to offer support. I thought it was strange at first. As a teenager, you hear what you want to hear during these serious-toned conversations. But this time, I listened. I tuned in. I even turned to look at him while he was talking. I can still see him—cool hat on his head and a cool lean as he drove. He told me to get involved in everything I could in school, to be successful at it. He said it was okay that I was a majorette (he really did not like the revealing outfits) and that I should do as much as I wanted to. He said he would help Mom support me financially. He said that he was glad to see me doing what I was doing. My heart leaps to this day when I remember that conversation. I did not know that it would be my last time seeing and talking to him. I am so grateful that I did not tune him out.

My brother was shot in the head by a jealous boyfriend of some girl who flirted with my brother in a club on the previous night. Apparently, my brother and this guy got into a fight, and my brother beat up the guy. The guy came looking for my brother that Saturday night and found him—pumping gas at a local gas station. According to eyewitness accounts, a car pulled into the gas station. The gunman leaned out of the passenger window and began firing shots in rapid succession. The car sped off as fast as it pulled in. While others ran for cover, it was too late for my brother. After several bullets were fired, one of them found their target as my brother lay motionless from a bullet wound to his head. He never regained consciousness.

The knock at the door at one o'clock in the morning brought the news that it was not good. I was the one who called my mother with the news. She left immediately for the hospital.

I was still alone with the girls, pacing the floor and looking out the window every other minute for my sister. Soon afterward, my sister arrived home. I told her the news, and she bolted for the door. She asked me to stay with the girls and leave the phone line open in case they called. I was still alone, unsure of what was happening, when my sister called around seven o'clock that morning to say that my brother had passed away. He was only twenty-two years old and had a child on the way.

This was the first time I had come face to face with loss and grief. Sure, we had other family members to pass away, but I would never know grief until this moment. I had to hold my tears (and grief) so I did not upset the girls. Little did I know that grief and isolation would linger from that moment and take up space in my heart and my mind for what turned out to be several years—not days, not weeks, not months, but years.

I held on to the last conversation I had with my brother. My memories of him became my motivation for doing just what he told me to do. Sometimes when I thought of him, I often felt like I was crying on the inside, like my heart shed more tears than my eyes could ever do. I needed to let go of the grief and release the isolation I felt from having to deal with my brother's death alone—while all my siblings were at the hospital. I did not realize how deep these emotions were locked inside of me.

And then one day, years later, it happened. I began crying and could not stop. I did not know what was wrong with me. I began hearing the words my brother spoke to me, but this time it did not trigger the same determination but rather brought a deeper, gut-wrenching cry that felt like everything in me hurt or ached. I now realize that God was purging the hurt, the grief, and the isolation. Everything came up. I was being healed. Even though I was not saved at the time or praying to

God for healing, it was God's way of healing me. God himself intervened when I did not know how to ask God for help. Now when I think about the last conversation I had with my brother, I feel empowered and grateful that God allowed me the opportunity to share those last moments with him. My heart smiles.

I learned that there will be times when grief and mourning present themselves, but they are not intended to last forever, or for a long time. It is difficult to move into the fullness of life that God intends for us when we continue to long for that which is gone or no more. We become stifled in so many ways—isolated, disconnected from so many and so much. Life passes us by, and we do not enjoy life as we should. Certainly we will miss our loved ones, but ongoing grief and mourning can impact our entire life. What I mean by that is simply this: if we live in a constant state of grief or mourning for that which is lost, we lose the ability to enjoy life in the present moment. We miss out on the joys of life that God has in store for us right now.

Jesus declared that he came that we may have life and have life more abundantly. God wants us to live and live an abundant life. Can you imagine how God felt when he decided to give his only begotten son, Jesus, to die for our sins? There is no amount of grief or mourning that is not felt or known by God. God knows our hurts. He knows our sorrows.

You may have experienced a deep hurt or grief that seems to linger in the depths of your being. It does not matter what brought on that grief. I know God wants to heal you and take the burden of sorrow from you. Release your grief to God, and let God heal you. God wants to free you and no longer allow grief and sorrow to linger in your heart. I believe God can put a smile in your heart as he did mine.

Remember that God stands ready to bless you. The joy of the Lord is your strength.

Thou hast turned for me my mourning into dancing: thou hast put off my sackcloth, and girded me with gladness. (Psalm 30:11)

Chapter 4

---◆---

GOD CALLED MY NAME

I will give you hidden treasures, riches stored in
secret places, so that you may know that I am the
Lord, the God of Israel, who summons you by
name.

—Isaiah 45:3

Do you remember the day God saved you, the very moment that
you completely surrendered and said yes to God? Did it feel as
though God lifted the weight of the world off your shoulders? Did
you suddenly feel free, at ease, encompassed in an indescribable
peace? Were you concerned about how others would look at you?
Would they believe you? Would they try to change you? Take a
moment to remember when you said yes to God and accepted

Jesus Christ as your Lord and Savior. Allow that moment of surrender and obedience to completely envelop you again.

I remember the day and the hour when God saved me. It feels like yesterday, although it was many years ago. I had graduated from college a year earlier and was living on my own. I had a good job and a nice apartment, but my life was in turmoil. I was fresh out of a long-term relationship but was sensing something was not right with my body. I was gaining weight, even though I was exercising like crazy. (More on this later.)

It was a Thursday night. My cousin stopped by my apartment that evening, unannounced. At first it surprised me because he never just stopped by without calling first. I never liked pop-up visits, so I had a subtle attitude to add to my surprise. I was watching television, and I remember him talking about the Lord and salvation, which I did not want to hear at the time. Perhaps he sensed it. He did not stay long but said what he had to say and left. I look back on that time now and see that God sent him to pave the way. He was the voice in the wilderness, as Jesus was coming soon to pay me a visit.

As I sat there watching television, I heard my name called. For a moment, I thought it was something on the television. The voice was soft, not harsh, not loud or commanding, but a soft whisper of sorts. I heard, "Denise." It seemed strange at first, so I turned down the volume on the television just to make sure what I heard was not coming from the television. And then it sounded again—"Denise." This time I got up from the sofa and checked the two bedrooms and the bathroom, thinking it was strange as there was no one else in my apartment. By the way, not at any time did I think I was insane. I really did not. I was becoming more alert by the moment.

I sat down again and turned up the volume on the television, thinking I could block the sound. Within minutes I heard my name called for the third time, "Denise." This time, I got up, went to the front door and looked through the peephole. Of course there must be someone at the door this entire time, and I just thought I heard them calling my name from within the apartment. I looked through the peephole, and there was no one there. I opened the coat closet (don't ask me why I checked the closet, but I did). As soon as I opened the door, a bright, blinding light illuminated the entire space. I was motionless. I could only see the brightness of the light. And then I heard the same voice speak again. He said, "If you do not give your life to me now, you will not have another chance to." I realized it was the voice of God. At that very moment, I knew the Lord was calling me—to salvation. He was calling me to surrender my life to him.

There were many times during church services when the invitation was made to give my life to Christ, when the "doors of the church were opened." I always thought that I should get up and go to the altar, but then I would justify not going. Each time the plan was to give my life to Christ the next Sunday. This time I was not in church. There was no altar call, but there was an invitation from Jesus himself. There was no preacher, no choir, and no usher, but Jesus called my name.

I remember the feeling of surrender. I felt the overpowering love of God that is completely indescribable but understood by those who have surrendered their lives to Jesus Christ. I ran to my bedroom and fell to the floor, saying yes to God, asking God to forgive me of my sins. I was crying, but my tears were tears of joy and peace. It felt like I was crying on the shoulders of someone who could lift whatever heaviness I was feeling. It was a release of everything that was wrong in my life. All at once I released it to someone who could change everything.

I was tired of trying to make my life fit my idea of what I thought it should be. I knew it was not what it could be, or what it was supposed to be. I knew there was something missing, a void even. I felt there must be something greater, something better for me. I needed more, and God had more in store for me. My yes to God was the release of God's peace, God's promise, and God's provision for my life in a way I have never known.

I could not wait to call my mother to share the news with her. She rejoiced with me. I could not wait for Sunday, to go church and make that walk to the altar and confess Christ before many.

I remember sharing my salvation with a close friend, the same person I was hanging out with just days before. I remember she cursed me out and told me that I thought I was better than her and that there was no way I could change overnight. At first, her response caught me off guard. I didn't expect her to totally understand, but I definitely didn't expect this girl to curse me out and go off on me. When God saved me, he immediately took the temper and profanity from me. The fact that I did not go off on her for cussing me out was proof enough for me that God had saved and changed me. The old me was a piece of work. The new me? Well, let's just say that I am not where I want to be, but thank God I am not what I used to be. This time I didn't care who ridiculed or rejected me.

And so my journey in Christ, as a new creature, began on a Thursday night, in my apartment, where I said yes to God. Remember that God can save you anywhere, at any time. Many people have said yes to God, and they were not in church. However, it is also important to find a church home and begin your spiritual development.

The greatest gift is salvation—a life in Christ. I only wish I had answered God's call sooner. Nonetheless, I am glad that I said yes to Christ. I cannot imagine my life without Christ. My life was empty and unfulfilled before Christ. Now I can seek God for greater meaning for my life, for his purpose and plan. I can go to God for answers and solutions that are more perfect than I could ever dream or think about. I can allow God to make me better in the areas in which I struggle. It is a feeling that I cannot describe, but I am glad that I can live it every day.

Is God calling you to surrender your life to him? Is there something in your life that he wants you to release to him? Trust God to mold you into the best you—based on his will, his blueprint for your life. It does not matter how good you think your life is right now or even how bad you think it is. I can guarantee you this one thing: your best life is in Jesus Christ.

Many times we think we will lose out on the things we enjoyed doing before we gave our lives to Christ. When you surrender your life to Christ, you do not lose anything. God has a much better replacement that far supersedes what you thought you had. Yes, you may lose some friends along the way. Trust me, God has plenty of people who he will send your way to be positive influences that strengthen and encourage you in your salvation journey. Trust God to give you what you need and who you need, when you need it most.

For I know the thoughts that I think toward you, saith the *Lord*, thoughts of peace, and not of evil, to give you an expected end. (Jeremiah 29:11)

Chapter 5

CALM IN THE STORM

My sheep hear my voice, and I know them, and
they follow me: And I give unto them eternal life;
and they shall never perish, neither shall any man
pluck them out of my hand.

—John 10:27-28

The battle for your mind is real. Let's settle that fact right now. God's voice is always instructing us to do what is right, what pleases him. However, the voice of the enemy is always trying to lead us down the wrong path to do that which is wrong, to please our flesh. When we listen to the voice of the enemy, we find ourselves justifying our decisions, reasoning within ourselves to try to make the decision "seem" right. If it is not of God, it is not right and will never be right. If it is contrary to the will of God, which is the word of God, then it is wrong. Plain and simple. We need to stop trying to make God's word fit our agenda but make our agenda line up to God's word. Then and only then do we win the battle for our minds.

It is a dangerous place to justify wrong thinking. It can only lead to destruction—one way or another. Remember I shared that before I gave my life to Christ, I knew something was not right in my body, and I was gaining weight. Let me finish that story for you.

I gave my life to Christ on a Thursday night. The following day, a Friday, I decided to call my doctor's office and make an appointment. I was gaining weight, even though I was exercising daily. I did not think I was pregnant because I still had my cycle—same time of the month, nothing out of the ordinary. Nonetheless, I needed to get checked out. I scheduled the appointment for the following Monday.

That Sunday before, I remember the feeling of excitement about giving my life to the Lord. After church, I was calling different family members to tell them about my life-changing experience. Many expressed how happy they were for me, and some did not have much to say about it at all. None of this deterred me because I knew that God saved me. I wanted God's plan for my life. I was different. My life was different!

Monday came. I remember it was an overcast, cloudy day. I went to work and left early for my 3:00 p.m. doctor's appointment. I told the doctor about my weight gain, especially my stomach, which was previously flat as an ironing board but started to appear a bit "puffy." (That's a better word than bloated or pudgy.)

The doctor suggested doing a pregnancy test. He came back with the results—I was about eight weeks pregnant. I remember him asking me what I wanted to do about it, and I can only remember saying that I needed to leave. That news sent my world into a spin.

I remember walking out the office into the pouring rain. I did not run. I just walked through the rain, getting drenched with every thoughtless step. I remember getting in my car, but I have no memory whatsoever of driving home, getting out of my car, or even turning the key to my apartment door. The next memory I have is sitting in my apartment on my sofa in total disbelief and the onslaught of an explosive mind storm.

The voice was loud, confusing, and demanding, repeating over and over with breakneck speed, "You can't have a baby. You can barely take care of yourself. What will people think? What will your mother think? You need to get rid of this baby. Yeah. Yeah. You can even have anesthesia, and you won't even know or feel anything. Get rid of it. Get rid of it." My head was spinning. The room was spinning. I could not see a thing for the tears that flooded my eyes and subsequently created a small puddle on the floor.

Suddenly, without introduction or a pause, another voice interrupted. Everything stopped and came to submission to this voice. This voice was not loud. It was not demanding, and it did not rush its words, but rather it was soft, soothing even, but very firm and authoritative. I knew this voice. It was the same voice I had heard just days before—the same voice that called my name. It was the same voice that echoed from the brilliant light. It was the voice of God.

Everything in me stopped and came to complete attention,

even the voice of the enemy. My head was no longer spinning. My heart was no longer racing. Even the tears stopped, and my eyes were clear. It was as though God himself stepped into the conversation from where the enemy left off, without repeating anything, and said, "And if you do, just as sure as you are on that operating table, under that anesthesia, I will take your life." *Boom.* That was it. That settled all confusion, all doubt, all fear. God won that battle. It was settled in the depths of my mind, my spirit, and my body. I would have this child and deal with whatever came of it.

I remember getting a greater revelation of that experience as the years wore on. It was not just a battle for my mind but a battle for my life. If you remember me sharing that God spoke days before that if I did not give my life to him at that moment, I would not have an opportunity to do so. I would later come to understand that God not only meant a spiritual death, but he also meant a physical death. You see, if I had not given my life to Jesus Christ several days prior, I can tell you assuredly God knew the decision that I would have made. However, he intervened just in time. He called me unto himself for eternal life in Jesus Christ. I cannot tell you how often I thank God for saving me when he did. I cannot explain to you how grateful I am to God for sparing my life—spiritually and physically. All glory be to God!

I remember saying yes to God during that mind storm. I remember asking God for forgiveness in that I was pregnant out of wedlock. I was not as concerned about what others would say or think of me. The only person I was concerned about was my mother and how it would affect her. I remember asking God to help me break the news to my mother because I did not want to disappoint her or break her heart. My heart ached at the thought of it. My mother, who sacrificed so much for me, who worked so hard for me, who supported me and my dreams, couldn't possibly take this news. I couldn't stop crying and cried myself to sleep that night on a tear-soaked pillow.

God woke me early the next morning, around two o'clock or so, and said very audibly, "It is well with your mother." I knew that voice. Here it was again, that same voice. I knew what that meant. God gave me peace in knowing that whenever I shared the news with my mother, it would not break her heart. She would be able to take it. It would not be too devastating for her. The heaviness was lifted, but nervousness took its place.

I remember calling home early that morning, speaking with my brother, and telling him the news. I asked him not to tell Mom because I would call her later and tell her myself.

Around eleven o'clock or so, I called my mother to tell her. I said, "Guess what? You're going to be a grandmother again."

Her response was, "What do you mean?"

And then I said it, the words that I thought I would say one day when I was married—the words that I thought I would be proud to share and tell the world. I told her, "I'm pregnant."

Her response was one of shock, "You're whaaaat? You're pregnant?" And then she said, "Baby, let Mama call you back."

My heart dropped. My strength left me. My eyes filled with tears as quickly as I gasped for my next breath. Nervousness was soon overtaken by explosive sobbing. This was not the way I expected it would happen. I thought God told me it was well with my mother, but instead, she sounded disappointed—not angry, but disappointed.

I felt sick to my stomach. I ran to the ladies' room at work and cried my eyes out. I looked in the mirror and said, "God, you said it was well with my mother. Why did you allow this to break her heart?" I did not understand it. It did not seem well with her at all. I couldn't take it.

About two hours later, I called my mother back. But this time it was different. She was different. Before I could say anything, my mother said to me, "Baby, it's all right. God said it is well."

She said what God said. That was it! A sense of relief, calm, and peace flooded my very being. The tears flowed like a river overflowing its banks, but this time they were tears of relief. My mother began to minister to me about what it means to be a mother. She shared some of the most heartfelt words that soothed me to my core. It was a deep love, a mother's love that engulfed me. Even though my mom was hundreds of miles away, I felt like I had just run into her arms and laid my head in her bosom. God showed up for me. He took the heartache of potential heartbreak from me.

I felt like I was on my way. I had received the forgiveness of God and the support of my mother. I had actually forgiven myself but felt that I needed the forgiveness of my church. I asked to meet with my pastor back home. When I met with him, I was very nervous. I did not know what to expect. I was a new Christian and pregnant out of wedlock. My pastor put me at ease. I was well received and spoken to with such love and support. God did it again!

The love from so many and the acceptance was nothing that I imagined, but it was what I needed. God paved the way for me. Yes, I made a mistake, but God showed me grace, mercy, and love.

It was settled now. It did not matter who did not agree or who did not like it. God forgave me. My mom forgave me. The church forgave me, and I forgave myself.

Perhaps there was a mistake you made or some decision in your life and you remember how God intervened. Perhaps you made a mistake and have not asked God to forgive you. Perhaps you are tempted to do something that you know is wrong. Just know that there is no temptation that is common to man that God has not already made a way of escape, a way that he has worked out for you.

No matter the mistakes we make, there is no need to try to cover it up, thinking we can hide it from God or hide it from anyone else. Just remember that nothing is hidden from God. He sees everything. God's eyes are everywhere, beholding the good and the evil. God already knows the end of the thing before its beginning. He knows the plans that he has for you. Admit your mistake.

When we come to God and ask him for forgiveness, he hears and he answers us. He helps us face our mistakes—head on. In most cases, it never turns out the way we envisioned but much better because God gives us grace to go through it. The one thing that is keeping you back from forgiveness is *you*. Go to God. Forgive yourself and forgive others who may be involved. Allow God to be the calm in your storm. God is waiting for you.

If we confess our sins, he is faithful and just to forgive us our sins, and to cleanse us from all unrighteousness. (1 John 1:9)

Chapter 6

TELL ME WHY

And he said unto me, My grace is sufficient for
thee: for my strength is made perfect in weakness.
Most gladly therefore will I rather glory in my
infirmities, that the power of Christ may rest
upon me.

—2 Corinthians 12:9

Have you ever wanted something so badly and thought you had
it or at least you were on your way to having it and then suddenly
it all changed? The very thing your heart longed for, what you
thought was God's plan for you, suddenly became out of reach.
If you are like me, you begin to wonder and question God about
why it happened and why you cannot have what seems to be his

will for you. I think it is okay to question God. Besides, he is the only one with all the answers. God is the only one who can give you proper direction, especially when you do not realize you are off course.

I remember many times questioning God about why something happened or why something did not happen. I remember the disappointment, frustration, anger, and many other emotions for not getting what I thought I was supposed to have.

I was five months pregnant at the time and starting to show it. I was still able to wear a lot of my normal clothes, but I was fast approaching the maternity aisles. I was sharing the news of my pregnancy with as many who cared to listen. I was about to be a young mother. It was scary and exciting at the same time. I tried to be careful about what I ate, but honestly, I think I ate everything that moved.

Around two o'clock one morning, I was thirsty and went downstairs to get a glass of water. Instead of turning on the light on the staircase, I sort of felt my way. I had lived in this townhouse for over a year and knew my way around in the dark, or so I thought. As it turned out, I missed the last step and fell directly on my backside, or more precisely, my tailbone. It was a hard, unexpected, and scary fall. I fell so hard that my tailbone was sore to the touch, but that was not the worst of it.

I knew immediately that this fall was not good for my pregnancy. I called the emergency hotline for my doctor's office. I was told to sleep with my feet elevated and monitor myself for any spotting of blood to make sure that I did not miscarry. I eventually was able to fall asleep, but I was uneasy about the entire experience.

When I awoke the next morning, the impact of my fall presented itself in the most dreadful way. The linen was bloodied. I literally screamed in disbelief, "This cannot be happening. God, please don't let this happen!" I was frantic; panic and fear totally engulfed me. I called the doctor, hoping to hear that it would be okay. The doctor told me to get in right away.

I drove myself to the doctor's office. I remember the office quite vividly. I could smell the cleaning agents and the smell of a hospital. The office was full of women who were near term, with bellies that protruded far enough to know that it would be any day now for them.

They did an ultrasound. The nurse never said anything about the ultrasound, about what was showing on the screen, nothing. She just looked at me with this sad, pitiful look and said she needed to get the doctor. I knew something was not right, but I was not prepared for my doctor's confirmation. The doctor came in, and she was soothing but direct. She said, "Ms. King, I am so sorry, but there is no heartbeat for the baby. I am so sorry that you have miscarried."

I let out a scream that echoed throughout her office. I do not know where it came from. I was not expecting the news, and I certainly was not expecting to feel the way that I did—completely empty. They wanted to sedate me because I was not taking it well. Instead, I needed to get out of there. I could no longer take seeing the other women with full pregnancies after hearing that I had just lost my baby.

The doctor suggested they do a D&C immediately because I could begin hemorrhaging at any time and it could be life threatening without medical help. I could not think of that at the moment. It was too soon. I needed to be with someone who could ease my hurt. I needed my mother.

I had just given my life to Christ a few months before, and I needed answers from God. I drove home and ran upstairs to my bedroom. My stream of tears increased as I looked at the bed linen and now understood what just happened. There was this protruding belly, but there was no baby. I kept hearing the doctor's voice: "There is no heartbeat."

I dropped to my knees and began to cry out to God. "God, tell me why. Why did you allow this to happen? Help me to understand why this happened. Give me something in your word. I need you!" And then suddenly, that same still, firm voice that I had heard months before answered me right away. While I asked for a reason, God gave me several. His voice was soothing and yet firm. He said, "First, it was done in sin. Second, your prayers have been for a healthy baby, and it's not your time yet." When I heard God's answer, an indescribable peace rushed in, as though God himself hugged me. I cried more but knew that I would be okay.

I called my mother and told her the news. She wept with me and yet comforted me at the same time. I needed to be with my family. Mom contacted my local doctor, who would perform the procedure in my hometown. However, I needed to get clearance from my doctor and the airlines. There were six people on a conference call making sure I understood the risk involved with me traveling in my current condition. I had to sign waivers stating that I would not hold the doctors or airlines responsible if a medical emergency happened in midair or en route to the hospital.

During the flight home, the flight attendants were instructed to make sure I checked for bleeding every fifteen minutes. Fortunately the flight was a very short one. As soon as I landed, I was rushed to the hospital, where the doctor and her staff were waiting for me. The procedure was a miracle, as my doctor would later share. I started hemorrhaging as soon as I was on the operating table. God spared my life—again!

God had a plan for my life that was being revealed. Yes, the loss of a child was quite painful. Even though I never got a chance to meet my child, it was still a life growing inside of me. Yes, I was disappointed that I would not be a mother as I thought, but I trusted God and knew that his plan was better for me.

Now, years passed before the added revelation of this experience. Remember how God saved my life and spoke to me about keeping my child? You see, God knew I would not go full term with this pregnancy. He saw something that even to this day I do not know what it was. But I trust him. I trust the answer he gave me, the reasons he gave me. At that moment, that very day, I stopped questioning God about that situation. I have learned to be content in knowing that it was good for me, that it was God's will. As hurtful as it felt, it was still better for me than what I could see.

So even through devastation, God has a way of showing us that his will is better than the thing we wanted most. I would much rather live in that peace of knowing that God is perfect in all his ways and his ways are past finding out than to live a life of regret, misery, and disappointment over what I did not get or thought I should have.

Our prayers should be for the will of God to be done and to be able to accept his will. Maybe there is something you need to let go of and trust God's will. Besides, we know in part and we see in part. God sees the whole picture, before it is even framed.

For his eyes are upon the ways of man, and he seeth all his goings. (Job 34:21)

Chapter 7

---✦---

MAKE THE DARKNESS LIGHT

For thou art my lamp, O *Lord*: and the *Lord* will lighten my darkness.

—2 Samuel 22:29

Have you ever had a time when you felt like crying and did not know why? Perhaps you cried and could not determine the reason for your tears. Have you ever felt mad and could not pinpoint the reason for your anger? There may have been times when you lost hope or felt like your situation would never change. I think we all can identify a period in our lives when we felt at our lowest point, when it seemed nothing was going right or as we felt it should.

We are pummeled with thoughts of failures, insecurities,

anxiety, and the list goes on. These thoughts rob us of our peace in God. I can tell you this one thing: the enemy does not want you to be at peace—not with yourself and especially not with God. That is why we are bombarded day in and day out with thoughts that are contrary to God's will. It does not matter the reasons why you feel that way; just know that these feelings are not of God but the enemy. God's desire is for us to live a peaceable life, to enjoy and experience all that he has prepared for us here on earth. It is not God's will that we struggle for our peace of mind.

Do you remember when God showed up for you in the midst of a mental storm? This storm can prove far worse than a typical weather storm. Why is that, you ask? Because it is continual, unrelenting, demanding of attention, and accompanied by rapid, thoughtless action. It thunders and roars in your mind all day and night. You go to bed with it, and you wake up with it. The things you should focus on become gray, overcast, and cloudy. You cannot remain quiet or still because a mental storm robs you of your peace.

I remember when God showed up in the mental storm of my life. I remember the day that felt like I was having a complete meltdown. Nothing was going right. The enemy's voice was so loud and so relentless in telling me that I couldn't handle the different challenges that I was facing. Work demands, financial demands, and relationship issues all seemed to bombard my mind and time. I felt as though I couldn't get a grip on anything. I was going in circles and dealing with the same stuff over and over again. To say that I was stressed out is an understatement.

The enemy seemed to be winning against me in the battle for my mind. I was slipping fast.

I was twenty-five years old, a young Christian. I knew how to pray to God for myself, but I needed reinforcements. God knew that too. I called my mother, sobbing about how it was all too much and I needed her to pray for me. At that very moment, my mother asked me to hold on. I couldn't believe it. I was in turmoil, in a crisis, and I needed help. How could she put me on hold?

My mother returned to the call with my aunt M.L. on a three-way call. My aunt M.L., who is no longer with us, was sweet as pie but a force to be reckoned with. She didn't play but had a soothing voice that made you want to just lay your head in her lap. When my mom returned to the call, it was my aunt's voice that I heard first. Her voice was soft, inquisitive, and comforting. At that very moment, it felt like God himself was talking to me as she stated, "Baby, tell me what's wrong."

Suddenly, it felt like something rolled up from my belly, burst past my throat, and blasted its way out of my mouth. I actually felt the moment of release as it moved up from the depths of my being, traveling with speed and force through me. I had no control; my healing was beginning. I let out a deep, deafening cry that encapsulated every single thread of anguish, heartache, and heartbreak and everything that troubled me.

As I told them about my issues, my hurt, and my struggles through loud sobs, it felt like time stood still. Neither my mom nor my aunt said a word. I thought it was a bit strange, but I was too busy being delivered and healed of all that ailed me. I rambled on from one thing to the next. I also did not know that my aunt

M.L. connected her daughter-in-law to the call to minister to me in song.

I remember hearing her voice and feeling this sense of awesome peace, calm, victory, and yet exhaustion. At the exact time she began to sing, my mind was clear. The words she sang were powerful and reached the depths of my soul. It was like God himself was singing to me, ministering to me in song until everything that concerned me shattered into a million pieces. Some of the words she sang were as follows:

I will make the darkness light before thee,
What is wrong I'll make it right before thee,
All thy battles I will fight before thee,
And the high place I'll bring down.

When thou walkest by the way I'll lead thee,
On the fatness of the land I'll feed thee,
And a mansion in the sky I'll deed thee,
And the high place I'll bring down.

The devil meant to destroy me. He was after my mind and wanted to cause me to have a nervous breakdown. It was as if God said to the devil, "Enough. Leave her and leave her now." Whew! How I love God. He is my protector, my bodyguard. He is my shield and buckler. The voice of the enemy stopped, and it stopped forever. I can say that I have never been under such an attack for my mind as I was that day.

I love the fact that I have several intercessory prayer warriors I call on in the heat of the battle. I feel better knowing that someone else is standing with me, believing God with me.

Oftentimes I feel better during the prayer or even immediately after prayer. I gain strength knowing that someone else is praying for me and believing God to show me his victory in the battles I face.

Perhaps you have weathered a mental storm and experienced the power of God that stopped the plan and voice of the devil. You know the feeling of relief and the refreshing that comes through deliverance. Continue to remember these moments and give God the praise for his amazing power that caused the storm to cease. Tell God how you love and appreciate him for not allowing the storm to consume you, for allowing you to weather the storm. Pray to God to continue to sustain you through difficult and trying life experiences that battle for your peace of mind.

Perhaps you are in a mental storm right now. You are reading this book and wondering how you will come through it. Perhaps every time you try to read your Bible or speak the word of God, you don't feel or see a change. Perhaps you feel your prayers are not being heard as the situation looks like it is getting worse instead of better. Sometimes it is hard to see God on the battlefield when you're in the heat of the battle. I assure you God is there. He will not leave you in the battle alone.

I encourage you today to find someone to help intercede for you and help pray you through this storm. Intercessory prayer warriors are powerful. Having intercessory prayer warriors is like sending a call on the battlefield for reinforcements, and they arrive just in time, ready and able to fight against the plot and plan of the enemy. They can carry you across the battlefield when you feel you have no strength left or when you feel cornered.

Sometimes that is all you need to regain your strength to stand firm in your faith in God, and then you are able to see God on the battlefield.

Ye shall not need to fight in this battle: set yourselves, stand ye still, and see the salvation of the *Lord* with you, O Judah and Jerusalem: fear not, nor be dismayed; to morrow go out against them: for the *Lord* will be with you. (2 Chronicles 20:17)

Chapter 8

◆━━━◆━━━◆

BATTERED AND BRUISED

Praise ye the LORD. Praise God in his sanctuary: praise him in the firmament of his power. Praise him for his mighty acts: praise him according to his excellent greatness ... Let every thing that hath breath praise the Lord. Praise ye the Lord.

—Psalm 150:1–2, 6

Each and every moment we breathe, we owe thanks to God. The next moment of life is not promised to us and can change in an instant. Certainly everyone would love to live a care-free, worry-free, problem-free life. However, we all know that at some point in our lives, we have met or will meet an unexpected, unanticipated event. Sometimes our very existence may be threatened.

You may recall a time when you walked away from a car accident that was far worse than anyone could imagine. Perhaps you had no injuries, barely a scratch, or perhaps your injuries were not as severe as they could have been. It does not matter the event for you to recognize that it was God who spared your life. The interesting thing is that these are the moments of which we are aware. What about the moments we never see—the unseen dangers that God keeps from us? The fact that you are reading this book at this very moment is enough reason to give God praise. You are still here. You have breath in your body to give God his due praise.

I remember one of my unexpected events quite vividly. My brother had just purchased a new car. Several days later, I asked him if I could borrow his car to go visit a friend. I had a car, but I wanted to drive the "new" car. My brother was cool about it but gave me what I thought was a bit of a lecture at the time. He went on about how we do not want to allow material things to control us and how it was just a car. He cautioned me to make sure that I wore my seatbelt (which I always do) because we could replace the car if something happened, but we could not replace me. I thought he was being a bit sentimental about the new car and really thought nothing more about the conversation. I assured him that I always wear my seatbelt, and out the door I went.

It was around six thirty in the evening on a weekday, and I had been driving on the highway for no more than ten minutes. The traffic flow was swift but not race car speed as it can be sometimes. I remember driving in the fast lane but not the far-left lane. I noticed that there was a flatbed truck in front of me with a load of what appeared to be junk—just a lot of stuff. I noticed there were two barrels on top that were the size of garbage cans. I fussed a bit about it because the driver should not have been in the fast lane or even on the highway with all of that stuff crammed on the truck.

I did a quick glance for the license plate and noticed there was not one. The thought entered my mind that I needed to get from behind the truck just in case something fell off of it. I did a quick rearview mirror check to see if I could change lanes. I noticed a tractor trailer, an eighteen-wheeler, was fast approaching to my right. I knew I would not have enough clearance to change lanes. And then, at the very moment that I looked ahead again, my concern became a near-death reality. It was as though it happened in slow motion. One of the barrels fell from the truck, struck the hood of my car, and then bounced underneath the car. The brakes locked, and the car swerved violently toward the median wall. The car bounced off the median wall and veered back into the flow of traffic. And there it was—the same tractor trailer I saw in my rearview mirror just moments before, but this time my car was heading underneath it. I could see the underbelly of the truck. There was nothing I could do.

It was as though my car had a mind of its own, and it was barreling straight underneath that truck. I remember thinking, *I am going to die.* I began screaming, "Jesus, save me. Jesus, save me. Jesus." I knew I would die. At that very moment, I heard glass breaking and the sound of crushing metal. I thought I was dead. I could no longer see, but I could hear and sense everything.

During the impact, I continued to hear the sound of breaking glass and crushing metal, and then suddenly everything went silent. No noise. No movement. *Surely I'm dead,* I thought. And then there was this bright light that appeared in the silence. As I got closer to the light, it got brighter and brighter. It was as though I was in a dream. It didn't seem real. I was in another place that I cannot describe.

I could not see or feel my body, but I knew I was awake, but where I didn't know. It was a peaceful feeling. As the light got closer and brighter, I saw the face of my deceased brother, Rickey. However, I felt like I was talking to my brother whose car I was driving, telling him over and over again, "I don't believe this is happening to me." I was dying, but I was not ready to die. I couldn't believe it. I was in shock. I had just had a conversation with my brother before I left the house. Was I on my way to heaven? I sure would have liked to think so.

Just as quickly as the bright light appeared, it was gone. At that same moment, I became consciously aware of my surroundings. My car was upside down. I was dangling from the driver's seat, held in by the seatbelt that was cutting into my neck. I realized that I was not dead, but started to panic thinking that the other cars on the highway would crash into me. Fear gripped with all its might. I knew that if I opened my eyes, I would be hit by one of the other cars that was on the highway behind me. I forced myself to open my eyes, and what I saw next was as much of a shock as the entire incident—a hole in the passenger window—my escape route.

I started a frantic motion of trying to unsnap the seatbelt. I was pressing the button, and nothing happened. I had to get out of that car. I needed to get out of that car. I remembered hearing a familiar voice, that same voice that called me by my name that day I got saved and that same voice that spoke to me many times since that day. It was the voice of the Lord. He said, "You're okay.

Look down." When I looked down, I realized that I had to press the seat belt button from the side to release it, which was different from my car, where I had to press the seat belt button from the top to release it.

I quickly unlatched the seatbelt and made a mad dash through the hole in the passenger window. I was knocking out the remaining glass with my fists and elbows to escape. I crawled onto the highway with immense fear of another car hitting me while I escaped the car. When I turned to look toward the traffic, I noticed almost a perfect line of headlights. Not one car was moving toward me—not one. As a matter of fact, they seemed far from me.

I made it to the shoulder of the highway. I remember a man coming to me and asking if anyone else was in the car. People started running to me and asking questions, but I could not speak. I could hear them, but nothing was coming out of my mouth. And then a lady approached me. She held my arms and began praying.

The last thing I remember hearing her say was, "Father, don't let her go into shock."

The doctors in ER were asking me all kinds of questions, trying to assess my pain and injury level. I had no injuries. The only pain I felt was in my neck from where the seatbelt caused a gash. Several tests later, it was revealed that there were no internal injuries, no external injuries, no broken bones, nothing. While I was in the hospital, one of the paramedics who transported me stopped by and said he had to see me for himself. He went on to say that he knew they were approaching a fatality when they came to the scene, but then he heard I was alert and well.

He said to me, "You serve a mighty God!" How right he was and still is!

Several days later, the lady who prayed for me paid me a visit. She said she had to see me to tell me what happened that night as she saw it. She said that she and her husband were traveling in the car behind me. They saw the barrel fall from the truck. She said her husband almost hit that same barrel and had to swerve to miss it. She went on to say that they saw my car swerve, and it literally went underneath the tractor trailer. Well, not completely. The hood went underneath it, but then the car pulled away. She said my car was being dragged by the tractor trailer because it was stuck to the side of it and then suddenly went airborne. It flipped three times before landing upside down. There was smoke and sparks everywhere. She told me that the other cars started backing up on the highway away from my car because they thought it was going to explode. Some people abandoned their cars to get as far away as possible.

She went on to say that suddenly they saw someone crawling out of the car. They thought it was a child. I was on all fours and crawling like a baby but moving really fast. She said the driver of the flatbed truck never stopped, but the driver of the tractor trailer came running back to the scene. He was screaming that he did not see me and thought that I was dead. When he realized that I was the one in the car and that I was alive, she said he lost all control and cried uncontrollably.

She said that I had to know how good God was and how he spared my life. I knew that already. I just did not know the whole story, which made me rejoice even more. I now realize why none of the cars were close to me and seemed to be in a perfect line. God kept them back—away from me.

I remember waking up the next morning after the accident. I thought it was all a dream until I felt the glass in my face and hair. It would take nearly two weeks for all the pieces of shattered glass to work their way out of my body. I looked in the mirror and began to remember it all. I started to get dizzy and could not open my eyes without feeling lightheaded and faint at every flashback—swerve, swerve, crash. The enemy was trying to take my mind now since he didn't succeed in taking my life.

I began to call on Jesus. I told God that I did not want to live a life of fear and instability or with mental issues. I asked God to give me something in his word to help me deal with the memories and the flashbacks. God answered immediately. I opened my Bible directly to Psalm 150, the same scripture that opens this chapter. My eyes landed on the verse, "Let everything that has breath, praise the Lord." I began to praise God like never before. Through my praise, my mind was healed and the plot of the enemy was defeated. My mind was free. My life was spared. I had the victory!

My brother came home one day after meeting with the insurance adjuster and seeing pictures of the wreckage. He asked me to tell him again how I got out of the car. I told him that it was through the passenger window and that I had to break some of the glass with my fists and elbows to get out. He shook his head and said that there was no passenger window. He said that the hood of the car was smashed all the way to the back seats. There was no passenger door and no passenger window. I can only conclude that Jesus himself provided an opening, a way of escape for me. I give God praise every time I remember this miracle.

My brother's car was replaced. I needed to be able to drive again without fear or anxiety. Several weeks later, I asked him to borrow it again so that I could prove to myself that I was okay with driving again. He asked me if I wanted him to go with me, and I said no, that I needed to do this on my own.

I traveled on the same highway, on the same day of the week, around the same time of the day. As I approached the accident site, I was sandwiched between two tractor trailers. My heart was racing. I was pouring sweat. I started to get cramps in my legs. I was fading fast. I began speaking God's word, "I can do all things through Christ who strengthens me." I repeated this over and over. Then suddenly, everything went away. No fear. No anxiety. No cramps. I was calm. I overcame fear and anxiety. I exited the highway and returned home. I won—again!

Every time we take a moment to remember what God has done in our lives, it should provoke praise. It should be that no matter what we may be dealing with today, we can press in and press past it to tell God how much we appreciate him and how much we love him for the many times he showed up for us and for the breath of life.

I think if we were to make it a habit to purposely remember, purposely recount the small and great things that God has done, it will cause us to see God in our present situation. I believe that once we see God, we see the situation differently. We see the thing already worked out. We see change before change occurs. Once we do that, we activate our faith. Once we begin to walk in faith, then we can see God show up like never before.

You may feel battered and bruised by life's challenges right now, but God is able to bring you through. I know it may not feel good right now, but know that better is coming. God is faithful. He will make a way of escape for you. Have faith in God to do it.

Now faith is the substance of things hoped for, the evidence of things not seen. (Hebrews 11:1)

Chapter 9

THIS IS IT

Now unto him that is able to do exceeding
abundantly above all that we ask or think,
according to the power that worketh in us.

—Ephesians 3:20

One of the big American dreams for so many people is home
ownership. It is something we work hard to achieve. Do you
remember the feeling you had when you bought your first home?
Perhaps it was an easy effort or perhaps not. In either case, I'm
sure it was a good feeling to provide for your family and have a
place to call your own. Maybe you are believing God to bless you
with a home. God is able to help you do just that.

There was a time that I moved from apartment to

apartment—one-year lease here and one-year lease there. In all of these instances, each move to the next place was always better than the previous place. However, I realized that there was something wrong with that picture. I wanted stability but found myself struggling to stay ahead or stay in one place long enough. I struggled financially and just didn't seem to get to the next level. I cried out to God one night and asked him why this was the case. God answered and told me that I was not faithful with the tithes and offerings. I asked God for forgiveness and to give me another chance to get it right. That night I rededicated myself to obey the word of God regarding tithes and offerings.

I was renting a condominium, and my lease was almost over. I did not want to renew the lease. I wanted to buy a house. I had just committed to doing what God would have me to do regarding the tithes and offerings. I prayed and asked God to bless me with my own home. I started to look for a house. I remember saying over and over again that the next place I moved to would be my house, the house that God had chosen for me, the right house, in the right neighborhood, for the right price. I repeated this over and over to as many who would listen.

The house-hunting process was arduous at best. I took to the trails to find the house that I believed God had for me. One of my best friends blazed the trails with me and my agent, looking at one house after another. Each house was always better than the last, but in the end, there was always something wrong with it— too expensive, too many repairs, or in the wrong neighborhood. In some instances we drove right past the house without ever stopping, knowing from a distance that it was not the house I wanted—far from it. Whenever I set my sights on the one I wanted, it was all I could ever think about, and then we uncovered something that proved it was not. We laughed plenty during those days at some of the houses I thought were the one. God knew I needed to laugh my way through the process as some days were more difficult than others, and who better than my best friend to get a good laugh in. The process took longer than I anticipated. My lease would not be renewed.

One morning I woke up in the wee hours to God's voice of instruction. God told me exactly where my house was located. He spoke the name of the subdivision. It sounded vaguely familiar. That was because several years prior, I was in the car with my brother, and he made a stop in that neighborhood to see one of his friends, a previous neighbor of his. I remember saying to him how beautiful the neighborhood was and that I would love to live there one day. God had a plan. He spoke that same neighborhood to me—now nearly three years later.

I called my agent and told her where my house was located. She looked it up on her list and said that the homes were too expensive for me. I told her that God said my house was in that neighborhood. She agreed to take a look.

We arrived in the neighborhood and saw a vacant lot where there was a recent house fire. That was definitely not what God had in mind. We continued and found another home that was for sale. From the outside, it looked really good. We got to the front door and the lock box would not open. My agent stated, "in the name of Jesus." We were determined to see the house God spoke to me. The lock box opened, and she retrieved the key.

As I stepped into the foyer of the house, the voice of God

spoke audibly and persuasively. "This is it," was all I could hear him say. I heard it three times. As I walked through the house, I kept saying, "Okay, I like this. I like that." I remember going up a separate flight of stairs to a bonus room. I jumped down the stairs, shouting, "This is it. This is it." I was saying what I heard God say. I did not know the owners had reduced the sale price of the house the night before. The new price was within my price range.

I had one week remaining on my lease, but the closing date on my house was two months away. I was not officially approved by my lender. However, the owners agreed to allow me to move under a lease purchase agreement until closing. I agreed because I knew this was my house. Nonetheless, God did not say a lease purchase; he said ownership!

I worked with the lender and provided all the information they needed. I paid off debts, wrote letters of explanation, stopped eating out, stopped shopping, you name it. I did whatever it took to make sure I was approved for the loan. This process also took much longer than I expected, and we had to extend the closing date. The owners were firm in stating that if I did not close on the new date, they would put the house back on the market.

The week of my closing, literally days before the scheduled closing, I received a call from the lender. She introduced herself and told me my loan was denied. Denied? Something was not right. I was at work, so I had to maintain my composure. I sat there numb for a quick second. I told the vice president that God was not pleased. I reminded her that I did everything that I was asked to do and provided full disclosure and explanations of my financial history. I told them that I was already in the house and would have no place to live. She apologized again and hung up.

It didn't make any sense. I had to go to God for understanding of it all. I got up from my desk and went to the ladies' room. I wanted to cry, but I couldn't. I was angry and yet confused. I looked in the mirror and told myself, "You will not cry about this. God will do what he said." I told God that I trusted him and asked him to do something about this.

By the time I got back to my desk, I had received a call from my loan officer. He was a bit frantic and wanted to know what was said in the earlier conversation. I told him exactly what I said— the same thing I shared earlier. He said the place was chaotic because Ms. King said that she was going to sue the company. I can assure you that I never said that. However, I'm sure God had something to say about the matter.

While I was speaking with him, another call came in. It was the same lady who had called earlier. She called back to tell me that my loan application was reviewed again and was approved. Yes, God intervened. Through lots of prayers and faith in God, I closed on my house as scheduled.

God wants to show you that he is bigger than man and that what he says goes. He wants to show you that he has the last word. No matter how difficult it seems to you and everyone else, it is not too hard for God.

Perhaps there is something that God promised you, but you were denied. You know what you heard God say, but it has not manifested yet. I encourage you to not give up. Trust God to bring it to pass. Go back and refresh your faith in God and do what he said. Go back and rekindle that dream, that goal, whatever it is. I promise you that if God said it, he will do it.

God is not a man, that he should lie; neither the son of man, that he should repent: hath he said, and shall he not do it? or hath he spoken, and shall he not make it good? (Numbers 23:19 KJV)

Chapter 10

HELP ME FIND PRAISE

Trust in the Lord with all thine heart; and lean
not unto thine own understanding. In all thy ways
acknowledge him, and he shall direct thy paths.
—Proverbs 3:5–6

There are times when we undoubtedly know that we heard God's
direction for our lives. We have peace about the decision and even
share it with our closest family members or friends. However,
when things go contrary and don't seem to work out, sometimes
those same family members or friends begin to question whether
you really heard from God. Perhaps the situation is so bad that
you too begin to question whether you heard from God.

I can tell you this: if God told you to do something, then do it. Do it and stand on what he told you. We don't know the full plan of God and can't ever see the entire picture. No matter how difficult the road seems, if God said to do it, then he will smooth the road at some point in the journey. Use the rocky segments as faith building. Remember the times that God allowed you to cross that rocky road and obtain the blessing he has for you.

Once I moved into my house, I started seeing all kinds of repair issues. I was completely overwhelmed. I knew this was the house God had for me, but the repair work was excessive. My brother suggested that I have the house inspected so I could have a complete view of what was needed. I know I should have done an inspection before I moved in. Regardless, God told me this was my house. Therefore, he knew the state it was in and what it would take to fix it.

I got the inspection done from the roof to the crawl space. When the inspector walked me through the detailed notebook that identified issues with the roofing, electrical, even the foundation, I cried and cried. I know you guys are thinking, *Man, she cries a lot, doesn't she?* I can only laugh at the thought of that. I am just glad that God sees my tears and wipes every one of them away. So cry if you must, but keep the faith until you see God!

I took that inspection book and presented it to God. I told God that this was *his* house. This was the house he promised me. I trusted him to provide for me so that the repairs could be addressed. I also provided God with my list too—painting inside/outside, new carpet, new kitchen counters, new floors, you name it. I felt that since I was believing God for repairs, I should believe him for replacement stuff too. So I created a list of everything I believed God to do in that house. I stopped crying and started believing God to do it.

Several months went by. I was working very long hours at work due to a special project. I literally left my home at six in the morning and returned around nine o'clock in the evening. I was working too much. I was exhausted.

As I left the house one Friday morning, I started to turn off the hallway light to the garage entrance. I heard God tell me to leave the light on. Not thinking much of it, I obeyed. On my way home late that Friday night, I remember saying to God, "Lord, I want to rest in on Saturday. However, I just need enough energy to clean up tonight, and then I can relax all weekend." (I absolutely love waking up to a clean house!) That was my goal. However, something else would change all of that.

It was after ten o'clock as I turned the key to the garage entry door. I could not believe my eyes. I stood there in total disbelief. There was water pouring from the kitchen ceiling. Huge chunks of Sheetrock lay on the kitchen floor, table, and countertops. Water ran through the kitchen and made its way to the very hallway that I stood in. At that moment, I remembered God's instruction about not turning off the light. It would have been the first thing I did, while standing in a pool of water and exposed electricity. I believe God spared my life—again.

I heard God say, "Get out of the house." I exited immediately and called my brother, shouting that my house had flooded. As I waited for my brother to arrive, I paced back and forth in my driveway, saying, "God, help me find praise in this."

My brave brother put on his rubber boots, flashlight in hand, and headed upstairs to see what was going on. He returned in haste with a solemn look to say that it was really bad upstairs. We called the fire department, the utility company, and everybody else we could think of. The power to the house was turned off, and the main water valve was shut off.

By seven o'clock the next morning, there were crews all over the place—insurance adjuster, plumbers, and contractors. Repair teams were everywhere. The repair team brought out a plastic bag to show there was a backup in my upstairs pipeline. A huge hair ball (not my hair, by the way) was stuck in the pipes. I left the faucet on in the hallway bathroom while I was getting dressed and forgot to go back to that bathroom.

At first, I was really mad at myself—for working all those hours, for forgetting something so minor, for the destruction that I now faced. However, the teams assured me that even if I left the water running, I should have just had a very high water bill that month as the water would have flowed through and not backed up. Remember, I was away from home for fifteen hours.

The amount of water damage was unreal. By the time the adjuster and the contractor assessed the damage, God arranged it so that everything that was wrong with that house would be repaired—everything.

God knew this all from the beginning. It did not take him by surprise. There is nothing that takes God by surprise. God may have told you to do something, and it may not be what you expected for your life. But I can tell you this: God can change anything and anybody. If you are willing to seek God, trust God, and wait on God to manifest the fullness of his promise, then you will see God move like never before.

Remember the other times when God spoke to you about

something that seemed to go contrary at first. When you look back on it, you see how God worked it out. It may have been a marital situation that was on the verge of divorce, but God turned it around. You knew that God said that was your spouse, but divorce was imminent, but God healed that situation. It may be a family situation, a job situation, your child, your business. Find praise in your current situation, and watch God bring it to pass. It does not matter what it looks like, feels like, or sounds like. If God said it, then that settles it.

I know firsthand that when we praise God, he lifts us above our current situation. God allows us to feel his peace and comfort during some of the most difficult circumstances. Through our praise we break through heaven's door and reach God in a way that moves him to come to our rescue. I'm talking about sincere, heartfelt praise, not the patty-cake praise. The kind of praise I'm talking about is that praise of reminding yourself of who God is until you begin to see him that way. It's that kind of praise that transcends the natural or physical place you're in and elevates you to a spiritual level of peace and confidence that God will work it all out. Praise God in the place you're in right now and you will see yourself in a different place later.

O God, thou art my God; early will I seek thee: my soul thirsteth for thee, my flesh longeth for thee in a dry and thirsty land, where no water is; (Psalm 63:1)

Chapter 11

GOD SAYS I'M HEALED

But he was wounded for our transgressions, he
was bruised for our iniquities: the chastisement
of our peace was upon him; and with his stripes
we are healed.

—Isaiah 53:5

When you are not feeling your best, you don't deliver your best.
You are not able to function the same way. You are not as effective
on your job or in your relationships. Sickness has never been a
part of God's plan. God sees us well, whole, and complete. I think
it is safe to say that we have all experienced some level of sickness
in our lifetime. It doesn't matter if it was a common cold, flu, or
something more serious; it did not feel good.

It is interesting to see how we tend to manage and shrug off the common cold and rarely look to God for healing. Instead, we may immediately think about nursing it ourselves, letting it pass, or seeing a doctor for further treatment. When a more serious illness presents itself, we may be more inclined to speak God's word over our situations or even run to God in prayer. But if you stop and think about it, God wants us to believe him for the small and great, for the non-serious and life-threatening issues we encounter in our lives.

Can you remember a health crisis that you faced and God healed you? Do you remember how concerned you were about the situation? Do you even remember when or how God brought about your healing? The answers to these questions are important because they help strengthen us for current and future attacks against our health.

God is the same yesterday, today, and forever. He does not change. He is the same God who healed you of the back pain and can heal you of the breast pain. He is the same God who healed your eyes and can heal your ears. It does not matter what condition we face, God can heal it.

I remember lying on the sofa watching a movie one night. I raised my arm over my head and suddenly felt a knot, a movement in my breast. I immediately began to feel around in that area and found a lump. I leaped to my feet and repeated the examination, thinking that perhaps if I stood up, whatever I felt would somehow not be there. It was there—a lump in my breast. It stunned me, consumed my thoughts daily, and even raged fear at the thought of something very serious. I scheduled an appointment to see a specialist. I did not want to see my regular doctor about it. I wanted and felt I needed to see a specialist. I sought the best in the region, but her schedule was booked. As expected, it would take weeks before I could be seen. My sister-in-law knows everybody and never meets a stranger. She has a knack for putting people at ease when she talks to them. And wouldn't you know it, she knew some folks in that office too! She made the call and talked to "somebody" who said they would squeeze me in. It didn't matter to me who she knew or who she talked to; I was glad that God used her and "somebody" to show me favor.

Now let me back up for a minute on this one. Weeks before I found the lump, I was in prayer during a drive to work. It was still dark out, and I was praying, singing, and thanking God for his goodness. During my prayer, I asked God to touch my body and cause anything that is not of him to die. Those were my exact words. I wasn't sick or anything. I was just speaking healing over my body. Now fast forward.

As I sat in the office of one of the best breast surgeons in the country, I tried my best to stay focused on the word of God regarding his promises for healing. Honestly, I was a bundle of nerves. My sister-in-law waited with me. Her presence eased my fears and helped to silence the voice of the enemy as she made me laugh a lot and encouraged me throughout the entire time. I felt better because she was there.

The doctor did a series of exams, none of which were painful. In the end, she needed to perform surgery to remove the lump so it could be looked at further. My whole body shook like a leaf. My sister-in-law held fast to her faith that everything was okay with me, and I held on to her every word.

On the day of surgery, I whispered a prayer to God. I told God that I trust him and that I needed him to help me keep it together. The surgery did not last long, but it seemed like forever as I waited anxiously for the doctor's report. What did they find?

The doctor seemed baffled. The lump was necrosis or dead tissue and was removed. The doctor questioned what could have caused this—did I injure myself or hit my chest against something? The only thing I thought of was the prayer that I sent up to heaven—God, if there is anything in me that is not of you, cause it to die. The lump was benign—no cancer. All I know is God healed me.

I speak healing over my mind and body on a regular basis. I ask God to shelter me from anything that is not of him. I was challenged for years with fibroid tumors, a condition that many women face. Sometimes these things grow so big and cause so much trouble that they have to be removed. Such was the case several years after I was healed of the lump in my breast. This time my doctor found a tumor that was inoperable. Based on the position and size of it, if they operated, I could possibly hemorrhage to death while in surgery.

Well, whose report will you believe? I believe the report of the Lord. God's report says I am healed. I asked God to allow this tumor to dissolve. I confessed that I did not want to be cut on again. I believed God for my healing. The situation intensified on many levels. I was put on bed rest. I couldn't go to work and had to sit with my legs elevated to keep this tumor from traveling out of my body. Yes, you heard it right. The tumor could dislodge itself and cause hemorrhaging and ultimately death.

I remember the day God healed me. My mom, two sisters, and I were in early-morning-prayer. While we prayed together often, we started praying in the mornings for our family and whatever else God led us to pray about. Each person was assigned a day and we rotated through the week. On this particular day, God gave my sister Vernita a prophetic word of healing for me. During the call, she instructed me to lie flat on my back because God said he was about to heal me. As she spoke the word of God, I felt the weight of what seemed like a hand rest on my stomach and press down several times. I was motionless and caught up in praise unto God. I knew at that very moment the hand of the Lord had touched me and healed me. The full manifestation of that healing presented itself not long afterward.

Several weeks later, I returned to work part-time and came home in the afternoons to rest. I did that for three days, but on the fourth day, something felt strange—really different. I didn't feel right. I got dressed. As I sat on the edge of the bed, I prayed to God. I told God that something didn't feel right. I wasn't in any pain, although some days the pain felt like the edge of a knife cutting into my abdominal wall. I asked God if I should go to work or stay home. I felt that if I went to work, I was just going for show, to make sure folks knew I was okay. However, my heart was not in it. I heard God clearly say, "Stay home." I obeyed and worked from home that day.

Around two o'clock that afternoon I finished a call with the team in Europe. As I stood up to go to the bathroom, I felt something drop like a huge weight or ball, and then I felt this warm, wet sensation. I looked down and blood was everywhere. I was hemorrhaging—the very thing the doctor said could happen at any time, anywhere, and without notice. I needed immediate medical help. I could bleed to death.

My brother called me at that exact time to say he would be away for a few hours. He and my sister-in-law were very good at checking on me every day throughout the day. I told him the situation, and he was there in an instant. We called 911. By the time the ambulance arrived, which didn't take long, my sister-in-law—yes, the same one who knows everybody—was able to reach my doctor. This was interesting because my doctor was scheduled to be out of town. How was she able to reach my doctor? Actually, my doctor returned from her trip earlier than planned. God gave my sister-in-law the wisdom to contact my doctor's office. Amazing God!

My doctor instructed us to come to her office, which was only a few minutes away, actually closer than the hospital. I thought for a moment, *What? I'm hemorrhaging here. Why would I not go to the hospital now?* The paramedics arrived, but I waived the transport. My brother took me to her office.

My doctor did a quick exam and confirmed the tumor had released itself and was trying to exit my body. We needed to go into surgery right away. Her office called 911, and within minutes paramedics were in her office, prepping me for transport. It all seemed so strange, but I was calm the entire time.

During the short examination in her office, my doctor asked me an interesting question for which I had an even more interesting response. When she told me the news that I was indeed hemorrhaging, she asked me if I was afraid. She didn't say afraid of what, but I knew what she meant, especially how she looked at me when she said it. Was I afraid of dying is what I felt she meant. My response was immediate, confident, and calm.

I said, "No, because the same God that made this body is the same God who is going to give you the wisdom to take care of it." With that response, she was ready to go.

While in the ambulance, I heard the paramedic telling the driver, "Go, go" which I interpreted as run every red light. She called the hospital and gave them all kinds of codes. She kept saying how sorry she was that this was happening to me. My response to her was that God is in control and I trust him.

When they rolled me into surgery, the anesthesiologist asked me a few questions. I told him that I wanted to enter into this surgery speaking the word of God over my life. I prayed God's word and remembered who God was to me. I remembered saying, "God, you are the faithful God. You are the keeper of covenant and mercy to them that love you and keep your commandments, even unto a thousand generations." By the time the IV started, I don't know what I was saying, but they later told me that I started saying, "The Lord is my shepherd," and then I was out.

Before I was rushed to the ER, I spoke to my mom and told her I was okay. How I thank God for my mother! Her loving words and tender voice can soothe anything that is wrong with me. I didn't know that my best friend reached out to my mom and secured an immediate flight for her. She handled everything and blessed my mom to be with me. God used her to bring the very person to my side that I needed most—my mother.

The nurses were wheeling me from recovery to my room. I was groggy and out of it but could still hear some of their conversation. I heard one of them say that they were taking me to Oncology 7. I could barely open my eyes, but I could hear and my thoughts began to run wild. *Nooooo, this is not cancer. It can't be.* I tried to process it, but it made no sense because I know God healed me. How could this be cancer? Was I dreaming?

When the elevator doors opened, I heard a familiar laughter, a familiar voice even. It was the voice of my mother, chatting with the nurses and staff. She was here! Already? My mind couldn't quite comprehend it. Was I in surgery that long? Was it the next day? Suddenly, I calmed down. My mother's voice calmed me again. I realized that if something was really wrong with me, my mother would not belt out such a deep laugh. (I love her laugh, by the way.) Okay, I was all right. It had to be all right.

My doctor came in the room and told me the news. The inoperable tumor dislodged itself and was in a position where doctors were able to get to it, and all they had to do was clip it to remove it. There was no incision, no sutures. Remember, I prayed to the Lord that I didn't want to be "cut on." God answered my prayer. The biopsy on the nine-centimeter, almost ten-centimeter, tumor was benign. God did it again. He healed me again.

You may be facing a health challenge at this very moment. I want to encourage you to believe the report of the Lord. Believe God's word. Make a bold declaration of his word over your life, and expect God to perform it. Know that God made your body, and he knows everything about it. Command your body and your mind to align with the word of God.

It doesn't matter how long you have suffered or the magnitude of your issue. God is able to heal you. Get a prayer partner, someone who can bombard heaven with you, someone who can carry you to the throne of grace when you are unable to pray for yourself. You gain power and peace through the prayers of others.

I know it may feel scary and overwhelming at times. I know

that you question why you have to endure the suffering. I know that sometimes you may get angry with others and even God. I can assure you that none of it takes God by surprise. He knows what you're thinking beyond the words you speak. God is the healer and stands ready to heal you. Put your faith in God who can do exceedingly, abundantly above all that you can ask or even think. Whatever you are dealing with, God can heal it.

Many are the afflictions of the righteous: but the *Lord* delivereth him out of them all. (Psalm 34:19)

Chapter 12

❖————❖————❖

MAKE ME BETTER

Behold, I will do a new thing; now it shall spring
forth; shall ye not know it? I will even make a way
in the wilderness, and rivers in the desert.

—Isaiah 43:19

I think we can all do a self-examination of our lives and see areas in which we need to do better. We should all strive to be better, do better, and have better. God has better for us, better than anything we can ever imagine or hope for.

Just because we have good jobs, nice houses, or nice things does not mean we have "arrived." It simply means we should be grateful for all that God has given us. God often blesses us with things we didn't even ask or pray about. God knows what we need. He knows the very thing that will help us get to that next place. God wants his best for us. I cannot say this enough. God wants to see us successful. God wants to see us fruitful. However, God does not want the things to have us, where we are drawn away from him because of them.

God knows every area of lack, inefficiency, ineffectiveness, and insufficiency in our lives. It does not matter the area of shortcoming; God wants to make us better. He wants to reach us to improve those areas. He may send someone to mentor or coach in a particular area of skill or knowledge. It can be something simple or even complex. It doesn't matter to God because nothing is too hard for him.

Take a moment to remember a time in your life when you wanted to be better or do better. If you thought because you went back to school and got a degree that it would make you better, think again. Actually, it was God's doing. He wanted you to accomplish or succeed in that area. Perhaps you wanted to understand God's word better and so you started attending Bible study sessions or going to church more often, or listening to tapes or watching videos. Actually, that was God's doing too.

Very early in my career, I was so rough around the edges. I did not know anything about business or corporate America. I was still in college when I started my job that eventually lasted for seventeen years. I did not know anything about business etiquette, business communication, or any of that. I still had a profane tongue and a hot temper—I was not saved yet, but a year into my job, God saved me. When God saved me, the first things that went were the cussing tongue and the hot temper. It was interesting because it was like one day my mouth was so profane and the next day, nothing, no desire, no repeats, no slipups. He just took it. And I am so glad he did! However, there are still things that I definitely need God's help with and pray daily that he takes those away too.

God knew the plans he had for my life and he knew that I needed to be polished, groomed, and sharpened in so many ways in order to become what he has in mind. He made me intelligent and quick witted, inquisitive and determined. He knew that I needed help to birth greater in me.

Soon after God saved me, God sent a man in the name of Ronald D. Brown to join our company as the data center operations manager. Ron amazed me from the very first day. He didn't say much for several weeks. Sure, he talked to everyone about the job we were doing and the environment, but it was from a position of learning how things currently worked before he voiced anything about changes.

Ron called me Ms. King from day one. He took this twenty-something-year-old young lady under his wing and began to mentor me in every area of my life. He had so many axioms for life that made you think about your life and how you should make it better.

Ron exuded confidence and commanded the room in every meeting he attended. He was patient and respectful to all but had no patience for mediocrity or laziness. This tall man was no nonsense and knew how to deal with delicate and complex matters. I noticed how well put together he was—well groomed, sharp dresser, and extremely intelligent. His vocabulary caused me to constantly jot down words that I had never heard and look them up later. I got comfortable enough where I started asking him to spell a word that I could not sound out enough to look up. He willingly obliged.

Within the first month of meeting Ron, he told me to work on developing my vocabulary. He instructed me to read books and highlight the words I didn't know the meaning of, stop and look up the meaning, write the meaning in the page margins, and then begin using the word in daily conversation. It worked. I remember my first word—lackadaisical. I used the word over and over again until I laughed at myself at how I overused it.

Ron gave me a list of books to read and a timeline to read them. We would have discussions about the books and what I learned from them. These sessions typically occurred during the lunch hour, so eating was sometimes a rare opportunity. I was being mentored and didn't even realize how impactful the changes would be in my life. God was making me better.

The more I learned, the more I wanted to learn, the more I wanted to be better, and the better I got. As a twenty-something-year-old, I didn't know much, but I was learning a lot now and I was loving it—most times. Ron was relentless in his effort to help me become better. He demanded my best effort and would not settle for excuses. There were times when I felt so overwhelmed with information, new learning, and his high expectations that I wanted to scream. I wanted to walk into his office and say, "Okay, I got what I need now, so I don't need to do that next assignment, or read that next book, or hear another saying, proverb or any of that." I laugh about it today because I can see myself going into his office and feeling that way, but once I was there, he imparted another nugget that got me fired up or pumped up all over again.

Ron's career exemplified his work ethics. He became the president of our company in a few short years. As he was growing in rank, I was growing in every area of my life. I had a greater understanding of who I was and what I wanted to do. I was experiencing better, and I liked it. I developed a thirst for wanting a better life for myself, for my mother, and for my siblings. I had dreams and goals and wanted to achieve them.

In all my years, I can say that God used Ronald D. Brown to make me better. God planted the seed and Ron watered the grounds. I know that God provided exposure, experience, and excellence in my life in a way that I honestly don't think I would have ever known except through the years of mentoring and tutelage provided by Ron.

Ron passed away suddenly in 2008. There are so many days that I can still see and hear him in some of the things that I do. I truly miss him, but I am eternally grateful to God and Ron for making me better.

Perhaps you can remember a special person or a significant time in your life that God stepped in and shifted your world to make you better. The desire to be a better mother, father, son, daughter, husband, wife, employee, business owner, friend, or whatever is birthed from God. God wants you to be better. Perhaps there has been no growth in a particular area of your life. Ask God to help you become better and to sustain you to do the things that will cause positive change. Remember how God did it before, and look to God to do it again.

If your desire is for better, for greater, for more, then seek first the kingdom of God. Seek God's plan for your life. It first starts with a desire to change—a desire for greater, for better, for more. God is able to bring you to the place in him, to the plans that he has already set for your life. Do you really want to change? Trust God to make you better.

For with God nothing shall be impossible. (Luke 1:37)

Chapter 13

RELEASE ME

> To every thing there is a season, and a time to
> every purpose under the heaven ... A time to get,
> and a time to lose; a time to keep, and a time to
> cast away.
>
> —Ecclesiastes 3:1, 6

It is amazing how we can continue to do the same thing over and
over, knowing that something needs to change, but not be willing to
make the change. Have you lingered in something that you knew was
over, that your time was really up? You may have longed for change
but did not know how to get out or move on. Do you remember
when God nudged you or made the decision for you? Perhaps it was
a job that was very demanding and stressful, lacked fulfillment or

a sense of accomplishment. Maybe you dragged through your day on that job until one day you were laid off or terminated. Perhaps it was a relationship that needed to end, but you weren't willing or able to end it. You were too comfortable with it. Your whole identity was tied to it. But then the other person ended it. You or others may have viewed these situations as unfortunate, but God intervened on your behalf and gave you that nudge in a way you didn't expect. You may have called it "a blessing in disguise" because afterward you were more relaxed and less stressed, more at ease with life, or at peace with everything. You found yourself more cheerful and outgoing and full of life.

There are times when God's nudge does not cause us to leap or cheer, but rather we grow fearful and worry about how to handle it. Sometimes there is heartache and pain as a result of the loss and the uncertainty of it all.

When God says it is time for us to move on, then we need to move on. We don't need to wallow in what we feel we lost when God is trying to take us to something better. I can tell you this one thing: the minute we begin to embrace the change that God allowed, the closer we move to something better. Sometimes we hold on to things that we should let go and in turn miss the things that are better for us. Sometimes we can't even imagine being happier than this present moment or having greater success than this present moment. We may question—can it really get better than this? When God tells you to release something, obey him. There is something more that he is trying to get to you, but that does not mean you will automatically or instantly see what it is. The fear of not knowing or not seeing your way from this present moment can be immobilizing.

I was on my job for seventeen years. I enjoyed the work, exposure, and experience, but as time passed, I deplored the politics. The company changed a lot over the years. It used to feel like a tight-knit family, but it evolved into a cutthroat, every man (or woman) for himself environment. The more new people in leadership positions were hired into the company, the more we lost in team building, synergy, and connectedness overall. The workplace was no longer enjoyable but a daily battle in one way or another.

There were some major organizational changes that totally wreaked havoc for many in the workplace. Most of it made no sense. I was too exhausted and too tired to keep fighting. I remember flying home one day and saying to the Lord, "God, release me from this job. I know that I cannot leave unless you release me." I was also in seminary at the time and figured I would resign and finish school. I did not ask him for another job. I just needed a break.

God woke me in the wee hours of the morning one day. He told me that he was releasing me from the job. He warned me that I would be asked to stay, but my answer would be no. He gave me scripture about Jacob leaving Laban's home and how Laban pursued Jacob. God had released me. He answered my prayers. The response was as God told me it would be. I held fast to what God told me to do. Had I not obeyed God, I would have accepted one of the generous offers to stay. I resigned and left my job. My plan was to finish seminary and figure things out as I went, but God had his own plan for my life.

Not even one month later, I stopped by my brother's house to have dinner. I was always forging for food at my brother and sister-in-law's house. I could easily find a great meal or snack there and still can—for the most part. What I found, though, was something totally unexpected. My brother had desktop computers all over the kitchen table. There were computer parts everywhere and no food in sight. I asked him what he was doing and what all this stuff was for. He told me he was building computers for a friend who was opening a computer lab for senior citizens at his church. I thought that was interesting. I asked him how he planned to deliver his product to his customer and if he planned to package his work to present it. We chuckle today at his response. He stated this was just a friend of his and he was just going to drive over and drop the computers off.

My response was, "No way. There is no way you will do it like that. You should treat this like a business. You need to document what he's getting and box each computer. You need to do a proposal and show the work effort that was taken, even if you are not charging him. You need a business license, and so on and so forth."

My brother wasn't having any part of it. He wanted to just build the computers, which he loved doing. He suggested that I handle the business aspects. I sat there and thought about it for a minute. Surely, if I could help generate millions for a company that I worked for seventeen years, I could do this. We prayed about it, and at that moment God gave birth to the business. God named it and put everything in motion for it. I had no idea that I would leave a company of seventeen years and within a month start my own business. It wasn't on my radar at all. I thought I would finish seminary and serve in ministry. Little did I know that there would be other ways to minister and run a business too!

Remember those computers my brother configured? God gave me favor with his friend, and he hired my company to set up their computer lab. It was my first client. I was so excited. It felt good. It felt right. I believed God to provide for the company and trusted him to help me be a blessing to other businesses.

I have been in business for fourteen years. Managing and growing a business is hard work. I have experienced the highs and lows, the good and bad. There are things that I know I do extremely well and things that I'm lousy at and must rely on others to accomplish. This is the vision that God gave me, and I continue to seek him for knowledge, wisdom, and understanding.

God knows the plans he has for you. They are plans to prosper you and not harm you. They are plans to give you a hope and a future. I encourage you to remember when God released you to the unknown of your future, but in due season, you were able to see the bigger and better picture that he had for you. You may be doing something today that you would not have ever thought you would be doing. You did not train for it. You did not go to school for it. God had it in mind for you because it was part of his plan to prosper your life.

Take a hard look at your life right now, and see if there is something you need to release to God or be released from. Be honest with yourself and be honest with God about where you are. If you feel unsettled where you are, ask God to show you what he will have you to do. God is willing and able to help you. Remember, you want God's release in God's timing, because in obedience, there is covering. You may not know what will happen afterward, but you can trust God to take care of you. God wants you to put all of your trust in him.

In thee, O *Lord*, do I put my trust; let me never be ashamed: deliver me in thy righteousness. (Psalm 31:1)

Chapter 14

A Way in the Wilderness

> He gave you manna to eat in the wilderness,
> something your ancestors had never known, to
> humble and test you so that in the end it might go
> well with you.
>
> —Deuteronomy 8:16

Sometimes we find ourselves in a dry place, a place where we feel like we are moving but getting nowhere. There is no growth, yet scarcity feels like it is ever present. The wilderness experience is not about money or not being able to pay your bills or have things. This wilderness experience can simply be a feeling of roaming through life, wandering from one place to the next, with no show of productivity or growth for the time you were

91

there. Sometimes you are released to this place on your way to God's promises for your life. Remember the children of Israel. Remember the forty years that were intended to be forty days. We can delay the promise of God for our lives when we don't trust God. There are times when we give power to fear, worry, or doubt instead of trusting God's word. God is so merciful in that he still provides for us, regardless of where we are. He uses our wilderness experiences to draw us closer to him, to build our faith in him, and to come out victorious in him.

I have had some really great years in business, some very lean years, and some very dry years. Through them all, God provided. God always showed up. There were times when I could not see my way, but God was my way. He is my way through the lean and dry times as much as he is in the days of plenty. What I am saying is that God will use whatever he wants to use and whoever he wants to use to get us to the promises he has for us.

God can turn things around in an instant, at the blink of his eye or the snap of his finger. I remember one morning when God told me it was time for me to open the doors of my company. He said, "This business will be a blessing to that father who was laid off from his job but stayed with his wife and children, taking odd jobs to provide for them. He said I would offer him employment that would bring his income back to a level that he once experienced." God told me to open my doors wide to that single mother who needed a job to care for her children and flexibility to pick them up from school. He said to open my doors wide to the elderly who had worked their years but now had to work in fast food and grocery stores to survive. He told me to train them and give them a place to feel connected again. God told me to open my doors to the college students who were trying to show that they could be great contributors to any organization. He said to give them a chance, to train them, mentor them, and coach them to their next levels. I heard it clearly and precisely.

I looked for office space for some time and could not find anything suitable. I remember God spoke in the middle of the night and told me to go back to my roots and that my office space was in a specific building. The building God told me was actually where I once worked with my previous company. I worked in that building for ten years and nearly ten years prior to the time God spoke to me. God worked it out, and I was able to move into that office space.

There was a problem though. I had very little office furniture. I remember saying to my team on a daily basis as we shopped around for office furniture, "God has one person who has all the office furniture we need. God is going to provide for us everything we need." We walked through that office regularly declaring the promises of God and speaking the word of God.

The day we moved into the office space, God revealed his plan. The company that moved us was not only a moving company but also sold office furniture. God had me call the owner, who was gracious to me. He allowed us to walk through the huge warehouse and select all the furniture we needed. It was exhausting but thrilling at the same time. I felt like my outward smile was as wide as the ocean because on the inside my heart was bursting with joy.

God knew that I could not afford all that furniture at that time, but he had a plan for me that was better and bigger than anything I could ever imagine. God later blessed me to pay for all the furniture through a bartering deal. My company provided training and consulting services for the furniture company, and we were able to offset our invoices. He blessed me through another business owner for which I am grateful. I often pray that God continues to bless and sustain that businessman for the favor he extended to me.

God does everything well. He is very detailed and loves order. My cousin was instrumental in decorating the office space. She worked tirelessly to find the right look, often sending me pictures of a wall hanging, plant, chair, you name it. We had many early-morning conversations when she was retiring for the night around three o'clock, and I was just waking up at that time. God revealed his plan for the office space and how to decorate it through us. I remember how we would literally burst with excitement when an idea came to us that we both knew, at that moment, was God-given. She was always on a mission to find the best of whatever. She was my blessing. The office was beautifully adorned.

I'm thankful to God for sending the right people to take that faith walk with me during that time. We stood on faith and the promises of God for the vision he gave and the provision that he released to support it. They stood in the gap many days and confirmed God's word in that office for every need we had.

I know the vision that God shared about the company, and thus I made God the Chairman of the Board. I asked him for direction daily. God wanted me to trust him with the big and the small decisions. I knew there was a lot I had to learn, and I trusted him to help me through.

What seems so interesting is that even with all of this, there still may be challenges. I think the challenges come so that we can trust God more, so that we can see our own inadequacies and go to God for help. I sure went to God a lot because I needed a lot of help. There is nothing wrong with admitting that. I never want to be in a place where I think I have it all figured out and don't go to God for direction, knowledge, wisdom, and understanding. That is a dangerous place to be.

When God gives us work to do, he will equip us to do that work. He will not leave us without help or hope. I'm grateful for the entrepreneur heart that God gave me. I don't ever want to take it for granted. My sole desire is to be a blessing to others and allow my actions and the intent of my heart be pleasing to God.

We must learn to trust God in the midst of our dry places as well as in the days of plenty. We must rely on God to water the soil, bring the sunshine, and make our efforts blossom so that he gets the glory. He is the one who sustains us when it seems like there is no support, no provision, and no growth. There are many companies that struggled in their start-up years, but God brought them to the top of their industries, and they are multibillion-dollar companies today.

It does not matter how you start but rather how you finish. Continue to trust God to provide for you in everything—even when it feels like the struggle is great and tiring, and even when it seems you are bursting at the seams from growth and success.

We must remember that it is not the power of our own hands that brings us wealth but the Lord God. It is God, has always been God, and it will forever be God.

Jesus Christ the same yesterday, and to day, and for ever. (Hebrews 13:8)

Chapter 15

FROM FAITH TO FAITH

But without faith it is impossible to please him:
for he that cometh to God must believe that he is,
and that he is a rewarder of them that diligently
seek him.

—Hebrews 11:6

I am glad that God governs my life, for if it were left up to me, it
would be a huge mess. I cannot imagine my life without Christ.
I cannot imagine my life without God's favor, grace, and mercy.
Everything that I hope to accomplish, that I hope to experience,
comes as a result of God's direction for my life.

I am recommitting myself to do the will of God. I know that
I am not perfect, and God knows that too. I just want his perfect

will for my life. I want to rise above thinking anything contrary to his word. I want to excel beyond mediocrity and complacency that may be found in my life. I want to think on the possibilities during impossible situations. I want to see myself as God sees me. When faced with challenges, I want to see God and not the challenge. I want to see God's power engulf whatever the issue of life may be. I want to remain calm when I see others panic. I want to be unmoved and unshakeable in my faith. The only way I know to see this desire become my reality is to stay before God, stay in his word, and believe his promises.

I encourage you to do the same. I encourage you to recommit yourself to doing what God would have you to do. Tear up your agenda and ask God for his agenda. Step back and ask God if what you are currently doing is what he wants you to do. If not, then find out what God wants you to do and start doing that. I guarantee you there will be an immediate change in your thinking. I am not saying that it will all feel good. I am not saying that others will jump on your bandwagon and applaud you for the change. What I am saying is that when you do what God has you do, then everything else must fall in line.

I hope that by taking this journey of faith with me you had a chance to remember God during the critical moments of your own life and praised God for showing up for you. I hope that as a result of remembering what God has done for you, you can stand firm and strong in your faith for God to work out whatever challenges you may be facing today. Thank you again for taking the journey with me. My prayer is that God will bless you and keep you as you continue your journey in the Lord.

So it is with much gratitude and honor that I thank God for

bringing this book to fruition. I offer God this book and this prayer of gratitude.

I Remember...When God Showed Up

God, I thank you that *you knew me before* I was formed in my mother's womb. Truly I thank you for never leaving me or abandoning me when I declared *I'm saved* and then turned away from you. I thank you for covering my grief in the midst of *sudden loss.* Thank you, God, for the day you *called my name* and called me unto salvation. I thank you for being my *calm in the storm* when my mind was overwhelmed. I thank you for answering my cry about the loss of my child and *telling me why* it happened. I thank you for *making the darkness light* before me and sustaining me from a breakdown. I praise you for your mighty acts when I was *battered and bruised* from what would have been a fatality in the car wreck. I thank you for blessing me with a home and allowing me to hear you when you said, "*This is it.*" I thank you for *helping me find praise* to bless you when calamity came upon me and caused destruction to the house you gave me. Thank you for touching my body and helping me to believe your indisputable report because *God says I'm healed* when doctors didn't know what to do. Thank you, God, for putting people in my life to help *make me better.* Thank you for *releasing me* from what holds me back so I can become all that you are calling me to be. I thank you for being *my way in the wilderness* when things were barren and dry. You brought me out and into the place of promise. Thank you, God, for allowing me to chronicle these critical events of my life so that I am reminded of your goodness and your faithfulness that takes me *from faith to faith.* I love you, Lord, and I give you all the glory, all the honor, and all the praise for who you are and all you have done for me.

Bless the LORD, O my soul: and all that is within me, bless his holy name. Bless the LORD, O my soul, and forget not all his benefits: Who forgiveth all thine iniquities; who healeth all thy diseases; Who redeemeth thy life from destruction; who crowneth thee with lovingkindness and tender mercies; Who satisfieth thy mouth with good things; so that thy youth is renewed like the eagle's. (Psalm 103:1–5)

Scripture References

1. Remember the former things of old: for I am God, and there is none else; I am God, and there is none like me, Declaring the end from the beginning, and from ancient times the things that are not yet done, saying, My counsel shall stand, and I will do all my pleasure. (Isaiah 46:9–10)
2. And they overcame him by the blood of the Lamb, and by the word of their testimony. (Revelation 12:11a)
3. Before I formed thee in the belly I knew thee; and before thou camest forth out of the womb I sanctified thee, and I ordained thee a prophet unto the nations. (Jeremiah 1:5)
4. Fear thou not, for I am with thee; be not dismayed, for I am thy God; I will strengthen thee, I will help thee, yea, I will uphold thee with the right hand of my righteousness. (Isaiah 41:10)

5. But Jesus said, Suffer little children, and forbid them not, to come unto me: for of such is the kingdom of heaven. (Matthew 19:14)

6. I will praise thee; for I am fearfully and wonderfully made: marvellous are thy works; and that my soul knoweth right well. (Psalm 139:14)

7. Blessed are they that mourn: for they shall be comforted. (Matthew 5:4)

8. Thou hast turned for me my mourning into dancing: thou hast put off my sackcloth, and girded me with gladness. (Psalm 30:11)

9. I will give you hidden treasures, riches stored in secret places, so that you may know that I am the Lord, the God of Israel, who summons you by name. (Isaiah 45:3 NIV)

10. For I know the thoughts that I think toward you, saith the Lord, thoughts of peace, and not of evil, to give you an expected end. (Jeremiah 29:11)

11. My sheep hear my voice, and I know them, and they follow me: And I give unto them eternal life; and they shall never perish, neither shall any man pluck them out of my hand. (John 10:27-28)

12. If we confess our sins, he is faithful and just to forgive us our sins, and to cleanse us from all unrighteousness. (1 John 1:9)

13. And he said unto me, My grace is sufficient for thee: for my strength is made perfect in weakness. Most gladly therefore will I rather glory in my infirmities, that the power of Christ may rest upon me. (2 Corinthians 12:9)

14. For his eyes are upon the ways of man, And he seeth all his goings. (Job 34:21)

15. For thou art my lamp, O Lord: and the Lord will lighten my darkness. (2 Samuel 22:29)

16. Ye shall not need to fight in this battle: set yourselves, stand ye still, and see the salvation of the Lord with you, O Judah and Jerusalem: fear not, nor be dismayed; to morrow go out against them: for the Lord will be with you. (2 Chronicles 20:17)

17. Now unto him that is able to do exceeding abundantly above all that we ask or think, according to the power that worketh in us. (Ephesians 3:20)

18. God is not a man that he should lie; neither the son of man, that he should repent: hath he said, and shall he not do it? or hath he spoken, and shall he not make it good? (Numbers 23:19)

19. Trust in the LORD with all thine heart; and lean not unto thine own understanding. In all thy ways acknowledge him, and he shall direct thy paths. (Proverbs 3:5–6)

20. O God, thou art my God; early will I seek thee: my soul thirsteth for thee, my flesh longeth for thee in a dry and thirsty land, where no water is; (Psalm 63:1)

21. But he was wounded for our transgressions, he was bruised for our iniquities: the chastisement of our peace was upon him; and with his stripes we are healed. (Isaiah 53:5)

22. Many are the afflictions of the righteous: but the Lord delivereth him out of them all. (Psalm 34:19)

23. Behold, I will do a new thing; now it shall spring forth; shall ye not know it? I will even make a way in the wilderness, and rivers in the desert. (Isaiah 43:19)

24. For with God nothing shall be impossible. (Luke 1:37)

25. To every thing there is a season, and a time to every purpose under the heaven ... A time to get, and a time to lose; a time to keep, and a time to cast away. (Ecclesiastes 3:1, 6)

26. In thee, O *Lord*, do I put my trust; let me never be ashamed: deliver me in thy righteousness. (Psalm 31:1)

27. He gave you manna to eat in the wilderness, something your ancestors had never known, to humble and test you so that in the end it might go well with you. (Deuteronomy 8:16 NIV)

28. Jesus Christ the same yesterday, and to day, and for ever. (Hebrews 13:8)

29. But without faith it is impossible to please him: for he that cometh to God must believe that he is, and that he is a rewarder of them that diligently seek him. (Hebrews 11:6)

30. Bless the LORD, O my soul: and all that is within me, bless his holy name. Bless the LORD, O my soul, and forget not all his benefits: Who forgiveth all thine iniquities; who healeth all thy diseases; Who redeemeth thy life from destruction; who crowneth thee with lovingkindness and tender mercies; Who satisfieth thy mouth with good things; so that thy youth is renewed like the eagle's. (Psalm 103:1–5)

Made in the USA
Columbia, SC
27 July 2020